The
Consultant's
Calling

Geoff Bellman outside his home and office

THE CONSULTANT'S CALLING

*Bringing
who you are
to what
you do*

Geoffrey M. Bellman

Jossey-Bass Publishers · San Francisco

THE CONSULTANT'S CALLING
Bringing who you are to what you do
  by Geoffrey M. Bellman

Copyright © 1990 by: Jossey-Bass Inc., Publishers
                      350 Sansome Street
                      San Francisco, California 94104

Library of Congress Cataloging-in-Publication Data

Bellman, Geoffrey M., date.
    The consultant's calling : bringing who you are to what you do /
Geoffrey M. Bellman ; foreword by Peter Block. — 1st ed.
        p. cm. — (The Jossey-Bass management series)
    ISBN 1-55542-253-5 (alk. paper)
    ISBN 1-55542-411-2 (paperback)
    1. Consultants. I. Title. II. Series.
HD69.C6B45 1990
001-dc20   90-53092
                                                            CIP

Manufactured in the United States of America

A BARD PRODUCTIONS BOOK

Substantive Editing: Patricia Galagan
Copy Editing: Helen Hyams
Text Design: Suzanne Pustejovsky
Jacket/Cover Design: Gayle Smithe Advertising Design
Typesetting: Creative Computer Network/Graphic Express
Production: Gayle Smith Advertising Design

FIRST EDITION
    HB 10 9 8 7 6 5 4 3 2
    PB 10 9 8 7

Code 9076
Code 9225 (paperback)

C O N T E N T S

Foreword

*C*onsulting is a much maligned profession and probably for good reason. For one thing, it is too easy to enter the profession. All it takes is the cost of some stationery and business cards, at this moment less than one hundred dollars. The term *consultant* is also used to cover a wide range of sins. Out-of-work executives call themselves consultants while they are between jobs, brokers of financial products call themselves consultants to mask their aggressive selling efforts, and, in general, when people take our money and we are not quite sure we got anything of value in return, we call them "consultants." The fundamental problem facing the consulting profession is that of integrity. This holds whether our consultants are internal to a company or operate on their own as external consultants. And in fact, the larger the consulting firm and the larger its reputation, the greater our distrust.

The Consultant's Calling is an answer to the problem of discovering integrity and value in the consulting profession. On its surface the book lists a hundred and one helpful hints on how to be a successful consultant; Geoff loves lists. But that is not the strength of the book. The book is unique and valuable because it is an unvarnished expression of the integrity and spirituality of its author. In its style and form, it is an example of the consulting/living philosophy that is advocated by its author. What Geoff calls for in his advice on how to consult he embodies in his dialogue and confession with the reader. This congruence, ensuring that words and behavior are of one spirit, is just what too often is missing in the consulting profession. The lack of integrity in consulting occurs when consultants exploit their clients by serving their own economic or self-esteem needs, rather than placing service to the client as the single-minded purpose of the engagement.

What this means for consultants is that the person is the product. Who we are when we are with our clients is the essence of what we are selling. Clients buy where they feel understood. Our response to clients during the sales call is their best indication of how we will function under pressure in the middle of a project. Clients push us and test us; our task is to stand firm, let them know who we are and what values and viewpoints we represent, and by doing this show them that they can lean on us. This book is a long paragraph on what this process looks like and how it feels. The book is homespun and folksy in its style, which lets us know that the person of the author is present. Once again, this has meaning not just because it makes the book easy to digest, but because its approach stands as a metaphor for the way consultants should behave with their clients. You may be sophisticated and elegant, and homespun and folksy may not be your style, but each time the unvarnished essence of a person shines through the written word, it creates a voice and song worth hearing.

In addition to the question of integrity, the consulting profession faces the challenge of joining the abstract with the concrete. It is one thing to see a problem clearly; it is another matter to act on it successfully. In a broader sense this is the problem with our lives. How do I take the values and beliefs that I have always embraced and express them in the day-to-day, moment-to-moment happenings of my work. This is a longing in each of us, and we seek it through our work with our clients. The irrational belief is that if I can help my clients live out their own vision, I will, through that process, have learned to live out mine. A good example of this is our longing for freedom. The lure of consulting is that through this way of doing work I will discover my freedom, my personal and work life will be balanced, and I can pick and choose the projects I want to work on. I will have my place by the sea and somehow will have rediscovered my soul. Such a grand illusion. The harsh reality is that most of the consultants we know are the most strung-out people we have met, racing from place to place, worried about the abyss of an empty calendar, and trying to act as if each client is their only client, even though they sometimes can't remember their last encounter. The illusion is that freedom can be claimed by changing the structure of our lives. Freedom is more likely to be claimed by acting as if we have a choice wherever we are, whoever we are with, whatever the task. This act of living out, implementing, our vision and purpose in the given present is how the abstract is made concrete. This is the fundamental message we offer our clients. Too often they don't act on our recommendations because they are waiting for something outside themselves to change. This is an expression of their helplessness. A consultant's primitive offering to a client is the ability to confront this sense of helplessness. The willingness of our clients to choose courage is what makes our recommendations usable; this addresses our problem of being relevant and useful. Geoff offers many paths into the center of this issue.

One other area that is woven into the fabric of *The Consultant's Calling* is the embrace of the irrational and unconscious aspect of our work. Organizations are a celebration of the engineering mind. They operate on rational models; believe in logic and data as a basis for decisions; and see change as a process of planning, installation, and constant monitoring. It is this exclusive belief in the rational that gets in the way of the very transformations they are seeking. Organizations are human communities, driven as much by intuition and feelings and archetypal urgings as by reason. Our clients need attention at both levels, and consultants, because they operate on the periphery, are in a great position to focus on the more elusive and intangible aspects of a situation. In a way we are required to be systematic about the irrational parts of work. Geoff takes the stance that consciousness of ourselves is the key to helping clients see clearly the light and dark sides of the challenges they face. This means that clients and consultants are in some ways mirrors of each other. Accepting this, valuing it, making it explicit is the basis for genuine partnership.

If you have gotten this far through the Foreword, you are going to enjoy this book. In philosophy it affirms the responsibility each of us has for our own life, and this is always hopeful, once we get over the initial shock. Geoff has invited us into the home that is his spirit and shows us that you can make a living being a mainstream radical. I have always thought that the world is changed by those with radical hearts and pinstriped suits, and Geoff is my role model. The book is a triumph of goodwill, wisdom, and a kind of humble midwestern practicality. If Will Rogers had given attention to the consulting profession, this is the book he would have written.

Mystic, Connecticut   Peter Block
February 1990

To my parents,
William Goodrich Bellman
and
Charlotte Elizabeth Peabody

Preface

*How do you thrive as a consultant,
contribute to the world,
make friends, and
become the person you want to be?*

This book answers this four-part question. On every page, the answers it provides bring you a life perspective that is larger than work. Life perspective is considered when deciding what work you do, how much of it to do, and how you are paid. It is considered when deciding how you get the work done, how you work with your clients, how you help them bring about change. This book expresses the belief that your life, your growth, and your happiness can be enhanced through your contributions to the world as a consultant. Before going any further, let's explore the meanings of the words *consultant* and *consulting*.

Consulting is a common action in the world, although most people do not call themselves consultants. Consulting may be as complex as working five years with an organization, helping to reshape its mission, strategy, structure, and systems. Or it may be as profoundly simple and important as helping a child learn how to tie a shoe. Expertise and helping others get what they want are central to both these examples, and to the millions of consultations that are going on at this moment. Consulting may or may not involve business cards, deadlines, money, contracts, or three-piece suits. But to be effective, it must involve at least two people—a client with a need and a consultant with related abilities and a willingness to help.

So consultants are people who, when asked, agree to use their expertise to help clients narrow the gap between what they now have and what they want or need. Those who offer help that is not wanted may think they are consulting, but they are not. Consultants have clients, and clients decide whether they are going to be clients or not. Successful consultants are made by clients seeking their help.

Clients engage consultants because they expect consultants to bring something to the situation. Clients may just want more brains or more ideas to add to those they already have. Or they may want different skills, a different perspective, or a different thought process. They recognize that they don't have it, they think they need it, and they contact a consultant who might be able to help.

Consulting must be one of the world's older occupations, if not professions. People have been giving away help for years. It is only recently that significant numbers of us have begun to collect financial as well as psychic rewards for what we do. Some of us regularly receive a paycheck from the organization we are attempting to help. Whether we are called analysts, auditors, researchers, or advisers, we are internal consultants. Others of us wander a larger marketplace. We seek clients and a living from the fees we are paid for the work we do. We are external consultants.

At one level, becoming an external consultant is as simple as declaring yourself one. There is no widely recognized certification or accreditation required, no respected body to pass judgment, no board review. One of the results is that the marketplace and the Yellow Pages (and the unemployment lines) are crammed with consultants. The marketplace decides who will make their living as consultants and who will not. This attracts those of us with a bit of entrepreneurial spirit and unnerves others who do not want to depend upon such a fickle employer.

This book is for declared consultants who want to learn how and why another consultant consults. It is for clients who want to understand better how to deal with their consultants. And it is also for all of you who are wondering whether this consulting life is for you—which leads us to the last word of this book's title: "calling."

The Consultant's Calling is about responding to the voice within, the voice that calls us to pursue meaning in our lives. The book recognizes the possibility, even the necessity, of achieving much of that meaning through our work as consultants. Given that we spend many waking hours working, doesn't it make sense to put those hours in service to a higher motive than the dollar? Given that changes, struggles, and growth are part of the human work experience, why not benefit from that experience in personal as well as profitable ways? Why not recognize our consulting work as an important path we are taking toward meaning in life?

The dictionary tells me that *calling* is "a vocation, occupation, trade, or profession." I like that definition because it is wide enough to include most people who work. People can be called to be painters, doctors, farmers, lawyers (yes, even lawyers), preachers, teachers, truck drivers, or consultants. The dictionary definition has the breadth but not the depth I am trying to convey as I title this book. That definition is not as compelling as I would like it to be. I think of my calling as work I love to do, work I choose to devote myself to because of the special meaning it has for me. It is work that answers an internal call to "personal greatness," to borrow words from Peter Block. That is how I see my work as a consultant and that is how I write about it in this book.

You and I do not have to be called to do this work to succeed in doing it. We can approach it as a (hopefully) lucrative diversion from what our lives are really about. We can commit ourselves to consulting because we choose to play the role of consultant in the large organization—a role that we leave at the office when we go home to our "real" lives. That can work, but it seems such a waste when there is so much to gain personally from all those hours we spend on clients' projects.

Some of us have been called but haven't had time to answer. We are so busy doing "it" that we have not paused to figure out what "it" is all about. Or the caller, whoever it is, is on hold; we intend to return the call . . . tomorrow. This book offers the possibility that tomorrow has arrived. Those who make the time to read this book can also provide the time needed to hear what their inner voice is calling them to do with the work in their lives. My experience shows that when I do not take time to figure out what I want, I am sentenced to doing what others want. This is an especially large risk for people in our line of work.

The subtitle, *Bringing Who You Are to What You Do,* can be understood from at least two perspectives. One reaction to it might be, "Do we have any choice? I mean, who *else* am I going to bring?" In line with that orientation, I believe that each of us chooses what we bring to this moment in light of our own particular circumstances. In that sense, we have no choice.

There is a second perspective that I would like to highlight. It has to do with the difference between the "me" I present to the people I work with and the "me" that is at work inside. Too often, those two "me's" are not in agreement with each other, and I do not act to bring them into agreement. Instead, I ignore the voice inside in favor of action. This book is about how *not* to do that.

I have read a number of books about consulting, have learned much from them, and I still needed to write a book of my own. I yearned to read more about how consultants lived their lives, found meaning in their work, struggled with their role. As useful as it was to learn about how to start my own business, market myself, contract with clients, and carry out the work, I was looking for something else. I knew that consulting success, narrowly defined and pursued, would not necessarily bring what I wanted. To be successful in this work I needed more than skills and clients and cash flow; I needed to make the work integral to the life I intended to live. I wanted to read about consulting from that viewpoint. So I wrote about it.

Among other things, this book suggests that:

- You are as powerful as your clients.
- You don't need to accept every client who comes your way.
- You can pursue your personal growth through your work.
- You can build lifelong friendships with clients.
- You don't have to work 300 days a year, or even 200, or maybe even 100 to succeed.
- Your presence and perspective may be as important as your skills.

Each of these sentences suggests that success is defined within the boundaries of life, not in the marketplace. This is not a pipe dream. Or if it is, I have been successfully fooling myself and others since 1977. That is when I became an external consultant and began learning about, developing, and living by the guidance in this book. So far, I have been richly rewarded *when* I have followed my own counsel.

My goals for this book are simple:

- I want to alter your perspective. I want to help you see your work in the world, and to see the world, a bit differently. I am confident that you will act on any new perspective you gain and value. I am not focused on building your skills, but on helping you see where and when to use the skills you already have.

- I want to add meaning to your work and life. I intend to stimulate your thoughts about how your work relates to the rest of your life. I will encourage you to become even clearer than you already are about your underlying values and how they can be acted upon through your consulting work. I want you to find work that is truly a calling, to consider the possibilities that come with making your work pivotal in your life's purpose.

- I want to add meaning to organizations, through you. We are caught in organizational structures and systems that too often mistreat customers, communities, workers, investors, and suppliers—not to mention the environment. Our organizational theory and application have not kept up with the needs of the world they serve. I see the potential for quite the opposite happening; I see encouraging signs that large organizations can be a central, positive force in reshaping our society. Through this book, I want to help you bring the needed changes about.

So this book is written for people who are helping change come about in organizations while they help change come about in themselves. "Change agent" is the jargon often applied to those of us who do that. Being a change agent is more important to appreciating the content of this book than the type of change agent you happen to be. I count among potential readers those who specialize in: systems analysis, auditing, financial analysis, management development, communications, public affairs, parenting, educational technology, policy and procedure, job evaluation, organizational development, leadership, work design, union negotiations, marketing, public safety, health care, organizational planning, legal affairs, management, environmental affairs, public policy, community organization, . . . and the list goes on. Many of these experts will not define themselves as change agents or consultants. But I expect that they all will find something in this book relevant to their work and life, regardless of their specialties.

My own consulting has centered on developing people and organizations; that will be evident in my examples and my jargon. In my early years in this work, I led numerous consulting skills workshops, often for consultants whose technical expertise was quite different from my own. Though we did not share technology, we had much in common when it came to accomplishing work with our clients. I expect that to be true for the diverse readers of this book.

Because I am writing about work I love, I am inclined to overdo it occasionally. In my enthusiasm for some of my ideas, I may sound (or even be?) prescriptive. Please dilute these prescriptions with ten parts water and take the "medicine" only if you really want to. I wrote this book partly because I am often told that I consult a little differently from many other consultants and people would like to read about what I do. I am satisfied to stimulate your thought and don't presume to know what you ought to do.

This book came about because my need to write another book coincided with the opportunity to talk about my theory and practice at an Organization Development Network conference. The session was attended by experienced consultants, consultants trying to break into the field, consultants working fulltime for organizations, and people thinking about becoming external consultants. In other words, it was attended by an array of potential readers of this book! In that session I again recognized how we consultants need to talk with and learn from each other about our work. Many of us gave up regular conversations with peers when we became independent consultants. So I began to write this book that converses with consultants about the work that many of us love and see as a central part of our lives.

It wasn't just our need to talk with each other that inspired me to write. More important, it was the belief that I had something to say that was different from the other books on consulting. This is where the life perspective comes in. "Everybody" talks about what this work has to do with their lives, but I could not find anyone who was writing about it directly. I decided to.

Throughout the book there are a number of stories that I have drawn from my work with friends and clients. While these stories are true, names and organizational affiliations have been changed. This allows you to read the story and ensures that no one's feelings are hurt in the process. It also saves me the laborious task of getting a number of corporate clearances.

I struggled with balancing my references to men and women, "he" and "she," throughout the book. A frequent comment on the early draft was that I used feminine pronouns far too often. My intentions are unprejudiced; I hope my writing communicates that.

Seattle, Washington   Geoffrey M. Bellman
January 1990

Acknowledgments

*H*undreds of people made this book possible; I recognize those knowing and unknowing contributors in the next few paragraphs. This book would not be in your hands without them.

When I finished the first draft of this book, I sent it out to the twenty-eight people in the following list and solicited their comments. What they received was designed quite differently from the book you are now holding. It would be an exaggeration to call it a book; it was more a loose collection of thoughts clustered by topic. The efforts of these experienced and unpaid contributors could be totaled in not just hours, but days. Their work reshaped my work: Chip Bell, Dann Boeschin, Mike DiLorenzo, Julie Fenwick-Magrath, Bob Formento, Bill Kaschub, Sheila Kelly, Marvin Kopp, Linda Mains, Bob Miller, Ken Murrell, Jeananne Oliphant, Kathleen Ryan, Marian Svinth, and Lucille Ueltzen, plus Boyce Appel, Frank Basler, Forrest Belcher, Paul Gustavson, Ned Herrmann, Peggy Hutcheson, Bonnie Kasten, Larry Lottier, Mac McCullough, Patricia McLagan, Carlene Rinehart, Bob Stump, and Mavis Wilson.

They sent back pages covered with notes that I sorted into a mega-manuscript close to one foot tall. I was almost overwhelmed by the help I received from these people. I used most of the ideas they gave me; you are the beneficiaries. Asking for their help was the smartest and most threatening thing I did in writing this book.

My friends in the Woodlands Group (the last thirteen people on the list of first-draft readers) have nourished me quarterly since 1977 when we have met to talk about growing people, organizations, and ourselves. They influenced this book profoundly.

While writing the book, I occasionally recalled the origin of an idea, remembering who gave it to me. When that fact was especially clear to me, I honored the individual's contribution with a note. More often than not I had no idea to whom I was actually indebted, though I knew I was in deep debt to many. There is nothing like writing a book to help you realize how little that is truly original you bring into the world. So if I "borrowed" something from you, let me know, and I will give you credit in the next edition.

There are some consultants from whom I learned a great deal years ago, back before I knew I would be following their path. I still find myself thinking about how Peter Block, Stan Herman, Jim Maselko, Geary Rummler, and Marvin Weisbord worked with me when I was the client. Each of them has been an explicit model for me in some part of my work. Peter Block did me the further honor of writing the Foreword to this book. I am proud to see our work associated in print.

I love to work with clients who expect me to learn along with them as we deliver results in their organizations. I have spent years learning with Ed Boston, Clare Coxey, Earl Goode, Bill Griswold, Marv Kopp, Allan Paulson, and Tracy Peterson. Our partnerships on projects have multiplied the rewards this work offers.

I know that this is beginning to read like the script of the Academy Awards ceremony, but there are even more people whose help I want to acknowledge. You perhaps have no idea how much human talent is brought to bear on the writing, editing, titling, marketing, coddling, scheduling, designing, printing, publicizing, and selling of one book. At least a dozen people have worked directly with me—they each had help to offer and knew how to offer it. In a few words, they are good consultants. Five of them work with Ray Bard of Bard Productions: Patricia Galagan, Helen Hyams, Suzanne Pustejovsky, Gayle Smith, and Sherry Sprague. Seven more work with Jossey-Bass Publishers: Rachel Anderson, Luana Morimoto, Patricia O'Hare, Steve Piersanti, David Roth, Laura Simonds, and Paula Stacey. I would have felt presumptuous to have asked for as much professional support as they have provided.

As much as I have learned about consulting to others from my clients and friends, my most significant learning has been with Sheila Kelly, my wife for over twenty-six years. She has led me in my learning and shown me ways to grow that I did not even suspect were there. I am a consultant, and a much better consultant, because of our marriage.

G.M.B.

The Author

*A*t the time you are reading this, Geoffrey M. Bellman is at least fifty-two and has been a consultant to organizations for at least half of his life. From his first professional position in business research and systems analysis, to numerous corporate jobs in the human resources area, to his present position as an independent consultant, he has worked as an adviser to management. Fourteen years on the payrolls of three Fortune 500 companies (Ideal Basic Industries, Amoco Corporation, and G. D. Searle & Company) moved him from Denver to New Orleans to Tulsa to Chicago, and provided the foundation for his consulting work.

In 1977, Bellman started his own consulting business in Chicago; he moved it to Seattle in 1981. Since going on his own, he has consulted in the private and public sectors both here and abroad. Recent clients include companies in telecommunications, energy, confectionary products, aerospace, finance, insurance, forest products, airlines, and utilities, as well as government agencies.

In 1986, Bellman wrote *The Quest for Staff Leadership,* a book for service and support function managers in large organizations. The book received the 1987 National Book Award from the Society for Human Resource Management, which recognized *The Quest* as the year's outstanding business book.

Bellman is a member of the editorial board of *The Training and Development Journal* and was its chairman for three years. He is a member of the Organization Development Network, the American Society for Training and Development, and the Woodlands Group.

Bellman received his bachelor's degree in business and economics from Gonzaga University (1962) and his master's degree in international finance from the University of Oregon (1964).

In his current work, he helps people and organizations work toward productive, shared visions of the future. This involves him in strategic planning, team development, work design, and large systems change.

Bellman and his wife, Sheila Kelly, have three recently grown children who occasionally live with them in Seattle.

Introduction: A Quest for Meaning Through Work

*F*or reasons I cannot adequately explain, I continue to believe that I am on this earth for a purpose. If not "for" a purpose, at least *full of* purpose. And I am not unique in my clouded intentionality. As hard as it is for me to believe, everyone else is apparently here full of purpose too. We are joined in our lifelong, human quest for meaning. My own quest has led me to believe that part of my purpose is wrapped around working with people and organizations as a consultant. Not just as a job, or even as a profession, but more as a chosen vocation or a calling. Consulting has become a way of becoming myself.

In this book I attempt to see work from a life perspective, especially the work of a consultant. I see consulting as my opportunity for self-discovery, rather than just a way to make a living. I believe that work, though essential to life, is not life. As important as work is to finding our individual meaning, it distorts us when it is out of perspective. This book is about maintaining perspective, keeping balance, in our work so that we honor our life purposes in our every consulting move. This results in actions that are different from the actions we take when we honor work, authority, money, power, tradition, or even friendship. It opens us to alternatives that are unthinkable when consulting is played as a game.

So there it is. I have given away the secret. You have yet to finish the first page of the Introduction and you already know what all the other pages are about. Yes, they will be philosophical and value laden, as well as practical. The practical parts are what make the book so long. These pages are planned to help you realize what your work as a consultant can do for you and the others in your life.

You are about to be covered with and basted in my perspective on consulting. That perspective will seep into your own as you read. Looked at another way, this is a kind of lopsided conversation in which I talk with you and you form your responses but don't get to talk with me about them. My hope is that you end up talking with yourself.

The consultant talking with you is a person who . . .

Sees this work as a central part of life
Would do this work even if it didn't pay money
Has no intention of doing any other kind of work
Sees this work as a primary source of personal growth
Loves to work on change with people and organizations

This consultant also . . .

Struggles to balance this work with the rest of his life
Wonders whether he is operating out of talent or ego
Regularly screws up
Tires easily
Gets discouraged
Wonders whether this is the path

All of these statements are true, and this book is about maintaining some dynamic balance among them. In doing so it sometimes soars to lofty, idealistic heights, dreaming about the profound cosmic changes that can be created in organizations. At other times it burrows into the minutiae of the daily doing of work, down to "What should I wear today?"

Though consulting has been rewarding for me in many ways, I want you to know that it is not easy! There are great personal struggles involved in establishing and maintaining a consulting practice. That larger life perspective I love to write about frequently eludes my grasp while I am doing my work. I have written about these difficulties here.

I will talk to you as I would to a friend who cares about me and my work, a friend who will accept both my bragging and my fretting. Sometimes you will hear me taking pride in what I have accomplished; one reader said that some sections of the book "swaggered across the page." Yes, you will find some, I hope discreet, bragging. At other times, you may find me being too self-critical; some early readers said I over-stated my "warts." My advice is to read what you want to read skip the rest. The book was not written sequentially and it does not have to be read that way.

If this book were a home, I would describe it like this:

Imagine that rather than just entering a book, you are walking through the front door of a home. You have entered a large living room filled with natural light that shines in from windows and skylights. To one side, three people are listening to someone play a piano. Across the room is a water garden with a lovely little fountain. On the back wall of the room is a wonderful series of large, framed color photographs.

They show people apparently on vacation and having fun. The room surrounds a staircase that descends to the next floor. You go down the staircase and reach a second level. On each side of you is a room, and through a doorway under the staircase you can see stairs going down to yet another level. The room on your left is an office; judging from the intensity of its two occupants, work is in progress. The room on your right is a small sitting room, inviting and comfortable, with two people engrossed in conversation. You now take the stairs to the next lower level. There you find a utility room with all the equipment needed to keep the house going—the furnace, the fuse box, the plumbing, the water heater, and a workbench with tools hanging on the wall above it. No one is in the room; you decide to go back to the living room, ending your tour.

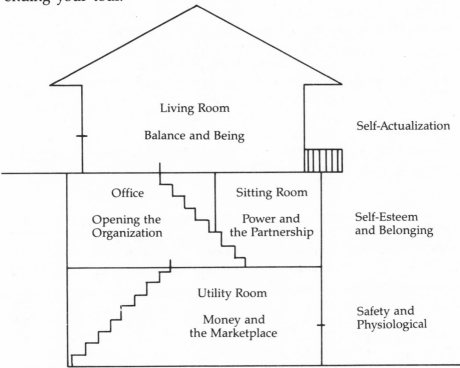

Like the home, this book is divided into four sections (rooms) on three levels.

In the living room, Part One: "Balance and Being," we devote lofty thoughts to our work's place in our whole life. It is filled with large and small ideas, all intended to help you set your work in your largest context—and then to act upon it.

The office is Part Two: "Opening the Organization." It focuses on getting the work done, consulting to bring about change in organizations. It explores what you can do to help the organization move from where it is to where it wants (or needs) to be.

The sitting room, Part Three: "Power and the Partnership," examines the relationships we build with clients as we do the work together. It is about the processes involved in maintaining equality with the client while we work side by side in the organization.

The utility room, Part Four: "Money and the Marketplace," is filled with the survival tools that keep the rest of our practice going. It is what makes the rest of the book possible.

Those readers familiar with Maslow's hierarchy of needs can see how it relates to the three-level, four-room structure of the home and the book. (*Thank you for noticing this, Marian Svinth.*) What Maslow would call *self-actualization needs* are the focus of what happens in the living room. *Self-esteem and belonging needs* provide the primary content of the office and sitting room, respectively. Basic *safety and physiological needs* are dealt with in the basement utility room. It does not sort out quite that tidily, but you can sense my intentions.

As I was constructing this book-home, a number of possible readers-guests came to mind. I have sorted them into seven groups. Look for yourself among them and consider my suggestions as to where you might start, based on which "room" is likely to be more comfortable for you.

Established, experienced external consultants. Readers in this category will find that almost the entire book talks about matters relevant to their work and life. If you think you are in the second half of your life, start with "Balance and Being." Everyone else start with "Power and the Partnership."

Not-yet-established, inexperienced external consultants. Start out in the basement with "Money and the Marketplace" to take care of some of your anxiety. Then move up a floor to read "Power and the Partnership." From there, it's your choice, but go up one more flight to read "Balance and Being" before you have been out on your own too long.

Experienced internal consultants. Though you will have to do some easy translating to internal thinking, most of the book's guidance is appropriate to your situation. Some of the larger perspective in "Balance and Being" is especially empowering for internal practitioners.

Experienced internal professionals considering becoming external consultants. Read it all, probably starting with "Money and the Marketplace"; it will help you imagine what life on the outside can be like.

Less-experienced internal consultants. Read the parts on the second floor, starting with "Opening the Organization" and then moving over to "Power and the Partnership." You may never want to go down to the utility room.

Clients trying to understand consultants. Read "Power and the Partnership" first, because it is about you as much as it is about us consultants. Then browse through the rest and see how it fits with your experience with consultants.

Everyone who fantasizes about being a consultant but doesn't really expect to be one. I think there are a fair number of you; I used to be one of you myself. Read the whole book and notice which parts you identify with most readily. Also note those parts that seem appropriate to you-as-you-are-today. This stuff isn't just for experienced consultants, you know.

You have had the quick tour and received my suggestions about where to start. I will now leave you to wander as you choose.

PART

One

BALANCE & BEING

*W*ork is a central part of becoming ourselves. Our work must be developed in balance with the rest of our lives for our lives to take on full meaning. This part of the book is for the part of you that attends to the balance in your life. We can visualize work on one side of a seesaw and everything else on the other. How do we assure that there is balance? What can we do in our work to infuse it with balance? What is the effect of work on our being, or our be-coming? What can we do to create the balance?

In a profound sense the rest of the book flows out of this

first part's larger life perspective. We care about how much work we do in relation to how it fits with the rest of our life. We concern ourselves with what kind of work we are doing as it relates to what we want out of life—at least that is the assumption behind what we will discuss here. This same perspective on organizations, client partnerships, and the marketplace is woven into the fabric of the whole book and receives special attention here.

This is not to suggest that we spend all of our time pondering the life meaning in every action we take. I am not trying to paralyze the consulting world with considerations of what a potentially profound moment this might be. I do believe that many of us who spend little time considering balance and being experience a pattern of frustration with our consulting work. So if you are one of us, and if these first few paragraphs include thoughts you seldom think, then read on! My belief is that our most profound decisions about consulting are related directly to our awareness of what we want to become.

This part contains two chapters. "Consulting: A Way to Live" is a collection of meaning-filled statements that profoundly affect the way I do my work. It is very belief and value laden, and is the more philosophical and conceptual of the two chapters. "Balancing Your Work in Your Life" gets down to the daily decisions and actions that allow us to become the kinds of consultants and persons we want to be. Expect some practical advice, useful questions, and specific guidance. As I reread this chapter, I was struck by how many little details are involved in something as profound as balancing work within life. Those of you who want to begin with larger life considerations will find food for thought here. Others should probably skip this offering for now and move to later, meatier parts of the book.

1

Consulting: A Way to Live

The Work

More Than a Living

Ask yourself the following questions:

If you were independently wealthy, would you still be a consultant?

Is your work a source of personal fulfillment or a source of income?

Is it possible to make a living doing work you love to do?

The way you and I respond to those questions significantly affects how we pursue our work. More positive responses define consulting as central to our lives. More negative responses explain consulting as a means to some greater goals. I will speak as one who finds fulfillment and contribution in consulting—and is able to make a living doing it. I do view consulting as a calling.

My starting point is the dream—the vision—I have of what I want to become in my life. This vision guides my choices. The vision includes finding significant growth and fulfillment through my life's work. Work is a most important part of my vision. I am not dreaming of the day when I will have nothing to do but play and relax. I am dreaming of the day when I can use my abilities without regard to whether or not I get paid, the day when I can seek out work entirely based on the potential contribution I can make to the community and the potential growth that work holds for me. This would greatly expand the world I now serve. I now find most of my fulfillment with the clients who pay me. It would be—it will be—freeing to move beyond that boundary.

Clients usually hire me for experience I have that relates to their situation; they want me to do what I know how to do. For my part, I am often attracted to work by the newness to me of a situation; I want to be paid to do what I haven't done before. It is ironic that clients are drawn to me by my experience while I am drawn to them by my lack of experience and the opportunity for growth. I want clients to pay me to learn as I contribute.

No, all of my work does not offer growth nor is it all "leading edge"; most of my work involves using abilities I have used many times before. This does not take away from the fact that I am most drawn to work that offers me growth. Think back in your work life to the times when you were most engaged, most stimulated to work. My bet is that growth was a major factor in those exciting times.

With growth comes risk. Because clients are involved, because they have provided the "classroom" for me to learn in, I have to deal with this growth and risk responsibly. My need for learning must be balanced with my need to contribute and their need for positive results. My need to risk must be balanced with my need for predictable results and their need to have confidence in my work.

This Is *Hard Work!*

I find this statement more true with each additional year I consult. In my first years of consulting, the possibility that this work could wear me out, use me up, was impossible to conceive of. The work was so exhilarating, so rewarding, that I could not imagine it consuming me. Now I feel differently.

The work is more rewarding than it has ever been. It is a most significant contributor to my growth; it gives me the opportunity to contribute to others. I continue to believe that it is good for the world. I cannot think of anything I would rather do. And it exhausts me. I work fewer days a year than many consultants partly because I need time to restore myself. I need the time off to re-create myself, to regain perspective, and to rest — physically, mentally, emotionally, and spiritually. The work consumes me at every level.

Mountain climbers don't climb every day and none of them spends an entire lifetime on the slopes of Everest. Running one marathon a month is unusual; running one a week is almost unheard of. As much as climbers and runners might get out of their "work," they do not attempt to perform constantly. They balance out their workload so they are not used up in the achievement of their ambitions. Whether we are climbers, runners, swimmers, tennis players, accountants, actors, engineers, or consultants, we must be reenergized to continue to do our work.

There is a special excitement that comes with pouring ourselves completely into an especially important project. I love to do that! I come out on the other side exhausted and, I hope, successful. I don't do this on every project or even most projects that I take on, but occasionally I invest myself fully; all other parts of my life are moved aside while I do this work. It takes on a special prominence for me as I test myself against the highest professional standards I hold. I am reaching for my own potential; I am attempting to become more than I have been before. I am making this exceptional effort because of what I will get out of it — not just because the situation calls for it. In fact, my exceptional efforts seldom occur because of what someone else asks of me, but because of what I ask of myself.

I recently worked very hard to help a group of elected officials resolve some difficult problems among themselves. They used me because I suggested it; it was not at all compelling for them. I doubted whether my work with them would help, but there was a chance, and the potential benefit to the organization from success was terrific. So I volunteered, worked very hard against great odds, and succeeded. That was most rewarding to me. The effort I put into it far exceeded what the client was asking of me. I will value that work for years because I grew through doing it.

I just paused to look around my office at the projects I will be working on during the next two months. I counted six projects I am involved in — six!! Any one of these projects would have been my most important single piece of work for the year, back when I was a corporate employee. Just thinking of them all at once tires me. Add to that three speaking engagements and related travel. This *is* hard work! This also is more apparent to me at fifty-plus than it was at thirty-eight. Naturally, I wonder how I will be feeling about this at sixty — and seventy? How will my investment in the work fit with the energy I have available? And all that is assuming that I am in good health.

My company does not have an elaborate retirement plan that was served up to me when I began working here. I have to take care of my future myself. If anything is going to be done about it, I must initiate, find knowledgeable people, make decisions. This is very easy to put off, even in the second half of my life. It was even easier to delay in the first half of my life when retirement and old age were still three hundred years away.

How much have you thought about this? What have you done about it?

The Self

Assessing Yourself

For us as consultants, it is especially important to understand who we are and what we bring to others, though this is not a bad idea for anyone wanting to live with intention. We need to be able to think about our abilities and talk about them with our clients so we can decide what work to pursue. We also need to know how we have prepared ourselves to reach for our life goals through our work. This means staying in touch with the primary tool of our trade: ourselves.

When I can step back far enough to gain perspective on myself, I notice that my self-assessment is quite consistent through time. I regularly give myself blame or praise for the same vices and virtues. My past training makes it easy for me to find fault with myself; I can build the debit list quickly, though I am reluctant to write it down. That same past training tends to block expression of my positive characteristics. I must remind myself that when I am talking with myself about me, I do not need to be falsely modest. My strengths will sustain me through difficult times, so it is useful to know what I will be relying upon. It is my strengths that will allow me to succeed in the work I do.

We should be able to look our strengths as well as our weaknesses in the eye. When others are interested, we should be able to articulate what we are, or do well, and what we are not, or do not do as well. We should be excited about what we bring to the workplace, thinking of ourselves as valuable resources to aid in what is happening. We also need the strength to sort out when we should not be involved, when our efforts would be better invested elsewhere. Confidence in our self-assessment allows these distinctions.

A part of how we see ourselves is how we think others see us. A match between my self-assessment and how others actually see me is useful. However, it is not as common as I would like it to be. Much more common is the match between how I see myself and how I *think* others see me.

For those of you wondering what to do about all this, the short answer is: Ask. Ask yourself and ask your clients how you are seen. Ask yourself both how you see yourself and how you think clients see you. Ask clients how they see you and (perhaps) how they think you see yourself. You tell clients how you see them and their work; turning that around seems reasonable. If the only feedback you now receive is whether or not clients give you new work, you should know that more information about you is available. Ask for it and use it to affect your personal perceptions.

Our livelihoods thrive on accurate readings of our clients' perceptions of us. I am not suggesting that we adapt ourselves to the way clients want to see us. No, we just need to know how we are coming across. It could be that our impact on the client is negative. If we know this, we can work with it. If we do not know it, we will work with what we have—the erroneous readings we have taken. All of this client perception "stuff" is graduate-level work; we first must have the foundation of a solid self-assessment to build upon. Our perception of clients emanates from ourselves.

> *What happens*
> > *when you release yourself*
> > > *to the powers?*
> *Discovery of a knowing you*
> > *wrapped too long in that person*
> *you had assumed yourself to be.*

Your Strength Is Your Weakness

This paradoxical truth is still emerging for me. When I consider where I might most need to grow, I am inclined to start listing my weaknesses, with the idea that working on a few of them would make me a better consultant or a better husband or a more complete person. There the gaps between what I am doing and would like to be doing are apparent and uncomfortable. Understanding the gap is a major step toward closing it, and a major step toward self-acceptance. I usually have a handful of these acknowledged gaps that I work on occasionally. This does help, as long as I am willing to put in the effort.

I also have areas in which I see myself as strong. My life experience, aided by others' feedback, helps me build images of strength. I celebrate many of these strengths just as I castigate myself for my weaknesses. And I move in my world in a way that accepts these strengths. Nevertheless, personal growth opportunities come out of corners where I do not expect to find them; my alleged strengths traitorously creep up from behind and stab me where I am most vulnerable.

Why is it that my major growth "opportunities" often come in areas where I already think I am doing very well? And why is it that the places where I believe I have pulled my world together are often those places where it starts to come apart?

An answer: My confidence in my strengths dulls my attention to their expression and their consequences. When I "know" I have a particular skill, I am inclined to put it on automatic pilot and concentrate my full attention elsewhere. Sometimes confidence in one's ability becomes overconfidence and produces unintended results. Here are a few examples:

- A consultant relates so well to his clients that they lose track of what is being accomplished.
- A manager who is extremely insightful and quick succeeds in turning off his entire staff by being extremely insightful and quick.
- A consultant is so enamored of her organizational model that she does not listen to clients' concerns about the model.
- An articulate and clever person dominates conversations with words and wit, leaving no room for others' contributions.

In each of these cases, a real strength led to unintended consequences. Each of these people was shocked to find that what he or she did so well was what in fact produced the unintended results. They overused their strengths.

The growth opportunity that comes from these quarters is as disorienting as it is unexpected. To find that a strength has become a liability can upset our personal confidence, disrupt our internal order, and put our egos in a tailspin.

This message is probably no more important for us as consultants than it is for others, but its application to us is particularly apparent. Clients hire us to use our professional abilities; sometimes these finely honed abilities hinder as well as help us. Excessive pride in or passion for our work creates distance between us and our clients, preventing the results we want so much to deliver.

There are good arguments for improving performance through recognizing and refining our strengths rather than just focusing on weaknesses. We should include our strengths when we are looking for areas in which we might need to develop. When we have a skill that we and others acknowledge, that skill deserves special attention, so that we can learn when and how to use it best.

Finding Your Uniqueness

Personal growth, authenticity, professional recognition, and financial success can all link with uniqueness. The opportunity exists to find these special differences about yourself and build your work life around them. Then clients will hire you to be yourself, to do what you know how to do and want to do. You set that up by building your business around yourself first, rather than letting the marketplace make the early decisions. There is more written about this in Part Three: "Power and the Partnership." For those of you who want to develop your thoughts on uniqueness, I have put together a ten-step process. You can use parts of it or all of it.

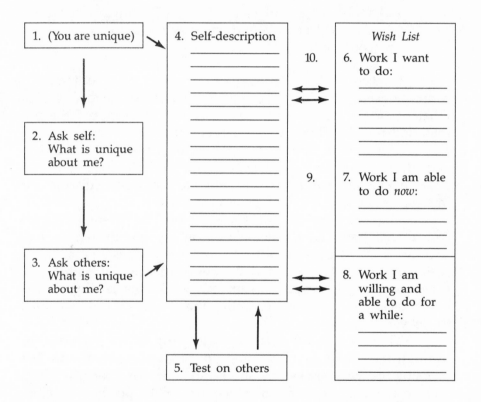

1. First of all, don't worry about whether you are unique; you are. I mention this because I'm familiar with the anxiety that comes with wondering, "What could be special about me?" If you experience this anxiety, you may be open to some positive actions that could reduce it. Be encouraged and move on to . . .

2. Ask yourself, "What is unique about me as a person?" Notice the question's emphasis on you as a person, not as a consultant. That comes later. We are starting from the assumption

that your consulting uniqueness will flow out of your personal uniqueness. In answering this question, list qualities, traits, ambitions, styles, goals, characteristics—anything you think might define what is uniquely you. Build a description so unique in composition that it just could not be anyone else. When you have "composed yourself," put your words aside.

3. Ask others, "What is unique about me?" Go to relatives and friends with the question and ask it in whatever words suit you. If you are uncomfortable with this, remind yourself that later on your clients will consider this same question.

4. Review all of your notes. Look for patterns in what you have heard from others. How do their comments fit with your own? What do you agree and disagree with? When you have collected all these thoughts about yourself, put them down in an organized way. It may be a list, it may be three paragraphs, it may be a drawing or model; it's up to you. Whatever you put down should express who you are in a way that distinguishes you from other people. Try to get it all on one page; this will help you distill your uniqueness to its essence.

5. Ask someone you respect to look at and comment on what you have prepared. Does it capture your uniqueness from their perspective? Test your work with a few more people. If what you have prepared fits you—according to you and others—put it aside and move on to the next five steps.

6. Now it is time to ask, "What consulting work do I want to do?" Write down what you want to do, regardless of whether you are presently prepared to do that work. Be as clear as you can about what you want. If you feel so inclined, you may want to write a few paragraphs about what a consulting week would look like for you five years from now if your wishes were granted. This is your statement of what you aspire to, your wish list.

7. Let's step down from the clouds to the hard pavement: "From the work that I want to do, what am I able to do right now?" Mark those items from your wish list that are within your current interests and capabilities. Notice how well prepared you are (or are not) to do what you want to do. For most of us, this list is shorter than the wish list created in step 6.

8. Draw a line at the bottom of your wish list. Below the line, add any work that you are currently capable of doing that didn't make it to your wish list. There are likely to be some things you know how to do and are willing to do now that you do not envision yourself doing long-term. For example, most of my early work was management training. I knew how to do it and didn't want to do it forever.

9. For a near-term comparison, put your shorter list from step 7 beside your self-description from step 4. How well does the work you want to do and are able to do *right now* connect with your uniqueness? Strong connections give you the opportunity to be your unique self. This is important to your motivation. A lack of strong connections between who you are and what you are able to do and want to do in the near term suggests that you take another look at what you will do right now. Reconsidering who you are is not likely to be fruitful. It is unlikely that you will be able to make major changes in yourself soon, so it is better to reconsider what you want. The additions from step 8 may help here.

10. A longer-term comparison: Return to the longer wish list in step 6 and compare it to your self-description from step 4. See gaps between the two lists as developmental opportunities that you can close over the next few years. You can close them by working from either list toward the other.

    • To affect the wish list, you can look more deeply into what you want; learn more and your wants will change, either lessening or deepening.

    • You can add to your present abilities by looking at what you want to do that you presently lack ability in. Identify areas where you can learn fast, supplementing what you already know. Ask more experienced people to help you identify what you might need to know.

    • To affect your self-description, build on the uniqueness you already possess, taking advantage of the qualities you and others already see in you.

    • The best way to expand the connections between your personal uniqueness and your envisioned work is by expanding your abilities, which also expands your uniqueness.

When we do the thinking involved in these ten steps, we are much better prepared to face the marketplace. Too often we jump into the marketplace, giving away our power and putting ourselves in a reactive mode with fewer options. Preparing before we step out into the business world helps us take advantage of all that it offers rather than being tossed about by it. There is a wealth of opportunity there! But the marketplace cannot care about us. We have to care for ourselves, prepare ourselves, and know what we want if we are to succeed.

Being Versus Playing a Consultant

Because the purpose of all this is to bring meaning to your life, a caution about playing roles seems appropriate. We all play roles and one I frequently play is "consultant." Playing consultant means doing what a consultant should do rather than doing what I want to do. It means pretending—speaking, listening, dressing, confronting, and acting in ways that are consistent with what clients expect. Fortunately for you and me, there are many ways to be a consultant. Our task is to define the consulting role with ourselves and our clients in such a way that it fits who we really are. When I can be myself and be a consultant at the same time, I do not have to pretend to be something I am not. When I do not choose to be myself, when I choose to "play" consultant, I have an extra burden to carry around. It is almost like a sandwich board with the appropriate behavior and attire painted on it—a confident smile, a clean shirt, and a pressed suit. If I am not feeling confident, clean, and pressed at the moment, the role is a burden. It may be a burden that I am willing to take on, but it is still a burden. Now, if this role burden is carried day after day, month after month, it becomes heavier.

My goal is to establish a consultant role for myself that is really me and then to "play" or be myself. Being a consultant is more comfortable than playing one. Even if I play the consultant role very well, it is still an act. It is still not me. When the costume and the script differ dramatically from what I am thinking, feeling, or being, I am clearly acting and not being myself. I have done this too often and it is hard to do. Consulting must provide me the opportunity to be myself often if it is to be fulfilling. I feel better about what I do and what I contribute when

I am being myself. Successful work is more solid when it comes directly from me, rather than through a role.

Role playing, in the pretending way I have been describing it, is focused on meeting others' needs while hiding my own. When I do this over a long project, I pretend that my needs are being met. When I do this in my life, my life loses its individual meaning because I am not giving expression to myself.

Yes, learning a new role can be an expansion of my basic self, but if I have to pretend while I am learning, my learning is reduced. When I am *playing* the consultant role and working with a client, I find it difficult to learn and acknowledge learning from my work. When I am *being* a consultant, I find it easy to learn and to acknowledge that I am learning from my work. In the first case, I act as if I know everything; in the second case, it is all right not to know everything. It's all right to learn.

The Fear

"What If . . . ?!?!?"

Our daughter, Tracy, used to ask wonderful "what if" questions. "What if we go off the cliff?" Or "What if the trees fall on our house?" Or "What if Big Foot jumps on the roof of our car?" We laughed because we knew how unlikely it was that the disaster she feared would happen. And our laughter was affected by the irrational fears we hold within ourselves.

I know many of those fears in relation to my work; I have at least a closetful. I will not risk opening that closet door wide (I'm no fool!), but I will open it a crack and show you what creeps out:

- What if they are calling but my answering machine is not working so I don't know about the call? What if the people who *want* to call me don't have my number? What if nobody is even trying to call?
- What if I am missing the point? What if I really don't understand what is going on here? What if somebody asks me a question at the meeting and I don't know the answer? What if I break down and cry!

- What if my talents have become irrelevant? What if all that I know was useful yesterday but isn't today? What if everyone knows this and no one is telling me?
- What if what I am saying that I think is so insightful is just drivel? What if I am not as smart as I think I am and I've just been lucky so far? What if I have just been fooling myself and some other people, and tomorrow they find out the truth about me?
- What if I screw this up? What if, as a result of my efforts, everything ends up being worse than it was before they asked for my help? What if lots of people are hurt in the process? And what if they fire me? And then they tell everybody about how bad I was! And they sue me! And my name is in the newspaper! And I am professionally disgraced!

And here are some contributions from friends:

- What if I didn't get it right?
- What if I have bad breath?
- What if it isn't perfect?
- What if I am dressed wrong?
- What if they are conspiring to give me bad data?
- What if my fly is open?
- What if they have heard all this before?
- What if their check bounces?
- What if my check bounces?
- What if they don't like me?

And what are your "what if's . . ."?

- What if _____?
- What if _____?
- What if _____?

The great thing about these "what if" questions and their disastrous answers is that you can always ask another one, leading to an even worse answer! (*Joel Flemming inspired much of what follows.*) As we pursue the disastrous responses to our anxiety-

ridden questions, we move through a tortuous series of embar-
rassments and humiliations to the ultimate separation—death.
We all know we are going to die, but most of us expect it to be
eventually, not in the middle of a consulting project! I use this
"what if" moment to conjure up fearful images of what is "really"
happening here. Those fears, which are rooted in my past—and
have no connection to this moment other than through me—
influence my behavior. And I suspect they affect your behavior,
too, which is one reason I am writing about this. It is reassuring
to find that other people have these thoughts, too. I hope you
have similar thoughts. But, what if . . . you think all of this is
stupid?

I frequently question what I do in my work and life and
some of that questioning involves the "what if's" I have given
here. When I am working with my clients, I try to risk in the
direction of being more open than closed about my self-doubts.
I acknowledge that the doubts exist and sometimes talk about
them in detail. In fact, most of the last few paragraphs contain
remnants of conversations with clients. I try to be honest with
my clients about these doubts without dwelling on them. I try
not to pretend conviction when I truly wonder about what I am
saying or doing.

I recognize that wondering, doubting, questioning, and
worrying are part of the process for people who are moving into
unexplored territory. I know that sitting around talking about our
fears all day does not move us forward. I also know that the
path forward is often blocked by these fears and that they must
be dealt with before the "real work" can begin.

Acceptance of the Darker Self

Fifteen years ago I denied the darker side of myself. When I
experienced darkness in myself, I saw it as an anomaly to be
eliminated. It was not part of the real me; it deserved to be excluded, neglected, or avoided. It certainly was not to be accepted
or analyzed or embraced. That has changed.

This "dark" discussion has everything to do with consulting. It has to do with power and acceptance and alternatives.
Understanding our many sides empowers us in ways that are
unimaginable when we only acknowledge one side of ourselves.
Accepting our darker side allows us to accept that side in our

clients. Said another way: If we do not accept our own shadows, how can we ever accept those of our clients?

I see myself differently now—to the benefit of my family, friends, and clients. I now acknowledge the darker side as well as the lighter side. I am still hesitant to look into this darker, negative, even evil part of me. But I *am* looking, because previous explorations have revealed that unexpected strengths come from this unlikely source. I am also looking because knowledge of this part of me serves me better than ignorance of it. I can understand and become myself more completely. I better understand and accept my anger, and that has led to new power. I better understand and accept my insecurities, and that has led to new risk taking.

In this view, we recognize that some of the forces operating within us are enlightened, positive, and constructive. We also know that there are forces in our shadowy, darker side that are negative in their inspiration and expression. Turning away from this dark side keeps us from understanding who we are and denies us access to what might be contained there. Turning toward this dark side is fearful and risky; we may lose control, or do something destructive. We may see something of ourselves that we dislike, even hate. We may learn more about who we really are.

In this view, good is not simply the absence of bad, any more than peace is the absence of war. We must work for and encourage good as certainly as we must work against destructive forces. Eliminating the problems in an organization does not produce a "good organization." Eliminating the sadness in our lives is not the same as creating happiness. When we let events take their natural course, we cannot count on the direction being beneficial *or* harmful. We always must attend to what is going on around us and inside us, recognizing the array of responses that are available.

These beliefs are part of the underpinnings of my consulting work and my life. They have a profound effect on how I see the work and the people I am working with. They preclude a naïve, "rose-colored glasses" view that expects projects to succeed because of people's goodwill and good intentions. They anticipate a spectrum of possible responses in organizations, people, and consultants. These beliefs are not pessimistic or optimistic; they are reality as I see it now. And they come with increased acceptance of that darker side of myself. My view of people is now more in line with my experience with myself and with them. I still expect a great deal of myself and others; I still hold positive assumptions about what people can deliver. And I have more room for disappointment, more acceptance of failure, than I used to. I do not blame "the culprit" as deeply as I once did—whether that culprit is me or someone else.

If you should feel so inclined, how do you get at this dark side? Now, that is a tough question to answer briefly (or even lengthily). Just writing about it scares me a little. It's as if my dark side is looking over my shoulder as I type, to see how honest I will be. Here are some alternatives:

Move toward your discomfort. Search out a part of yourself that has shown a pattern of making you uncomfortable in your life and your work. Seek to understand more about it.

Name it. Put a label on this part of yourself, and by doing so, legitimize it. Much as alcoholics name themselves for what they are at Alcoholics Anonymous meetings, so you can do the same: "I am an angry person!"

Let yourself experience what you are avoiding. Whether it is anger, grief, passion, sorrow, joy, love, lust, depression—whatever it is, find a way of getting into it that is not likely to injure you or someone else. Find a safe way of giving expression to it that goes beyond what you have done before.

Read about it. Chances are there are about a dozen books written by and about people much like you. Learn from them; enjoy the support they provide through their books.

Talk about it. Acknowledge that part of yourself to others. Not everyone at once, of course, but try it out on someone important to you. "I have been learning that inside me there is a very angry person." Or go to a support group that is receptive to your explorations of your dark side.

All of these alternatives have the effect of revealing you to yourself. They bring your dark side into the light. And in the light it is not as fearful. You can confront that part of yourself more directly than when it is back in the shadows.

Acknowledging a weakness, a secret, a dark part of me can be a step toward resolution. First I need to acknowledge it to myself and then I may be ready to acknowledge it to others. Acknowledging to myself is difficult because I have to become aware of the presence of this dark part of myself, a part that I have not been willing to look into. Chances are I have fearfully avoided it. I'd just rather not think about it, thank you very much! I am afraid that by looking at it I will lose some positive part of who I am, or that its darkness will swallow up the rest of me and I will be lost.

Moving beyond self-awareness to let others in on my secret brings a different kind of threat and opportunity. When I reveal something of myself that I have not shown others in the past, there is the possibility of complete rejection! There also is the possibility of total acceptance. And this could make it worth trying. If I gain the acceptance I dare to hope for, I can be myself with these people from this point forward. I don't have to choose to pretend any longer. A burden is lifted and I can use those energies that were intent on hiding me to reveal me, to be me.

Once I have acknowledged my darker side and revealed it to others, I don't have to behave in the old ways anymore. I can go on to something better for me. I can behave in new ways — that may or may not work. So new fears confront me: the fear of behaving in new ways and related fears about how well it will work. What if I do it wrong? What if it doesn't work? What if I screw it up? Another learning and growing opportunity. And here we go again . . . but what better is there to do?

I am aware of how oriented all of this is to personal growth and therapy. Frankly, I cannot think of anything we can do to grow as consultants that is more important than becoming ourselves more fully. We can load ourselves down with consulting tools and methods and techniques, but they do not operate themselves.

The Love

Love of Self

Love is not essential to professional success, stature, or recognition—though it can help. You and I don't have to love ourselves or our work to have clients or make money. The world has demonstrated this more times than we have cared to learn from. But if you want enjoyment, abundance, growth, opportunity, and a high yield on life, then love yourself, love your work, and love others.

Loving yourself comes first. Not first in the sense of mastery, but in the sense that this is where you start and finish and where you will be working for many years in between. Love of self is what opens you to loving work and others. How many times have I found that what was blocking me with others was something I was having difficulties accepting in myself? About 11,285.

> *I strike a pose to catch the light.*
> *Now, See . . . Appreciate.*
> *This is my best side*
> *To you, my only side . . . I imagine.*
> *Wait. Look away while I adjust myself.*
> *Do not grow impatient while I hide;*
> *It is worth the wait to see my best side.*

I must move through a knowing to an understanding of myself, an acceptance of what I understand, an embracing of what I accept, and a loving of what I embrace. When this has been done completely, I can love myself. More realistically for me, I am always working at new understandings of who I am and what I mean. I am always struggling to accept some parts of myself. I embrace a lot that I am and distance myself from other parts of me. And I love much more of myself than I used to but still have pieces I don't want to look at, much less love. And I know where much of the work within myself is yet to be done.

Love of Work

It is wonderful to hear someone say, "I love my work!"—whether they are clients or fellow consultants. I wish more of us were saying it and I am convinced that more of us could love our work if we allowed ourselves to. Many people wouldn't even have to leave their present work to love it; they would just have to change their perspective on it. They have been too busy complaining about it to recognize that they get a great deal out of doing this work each day. Others would have to leave what they are doing and face the uncertainty of moving to a happier but unfamiliar job.

If you don't love your work, and have not found elements of it to love for many months or years, then get out of it. Life is too important and work is too important to life to spend years doing something you do not want to be doing. Extenuating circumstances certainly affect your decision, but try not to use a child's education or a parent's illness as the excuse to continue doing work you can't stand. Aim higher and consider how you would go about getting work that you would love to do. This consideration is not a commitment. After you've decided what you would love to do, you can decide whether you are going to do anything about it. Do not block yourself from thinking about it; you may never learn what you didn't allow yourself to think about. Know that when you say, "I cannot quit doing this," you are saying, "I cannot change." You have defined your own powerlessness.

The marketplace encourages us to define the kind of work we would like to do and then go out to find clients who provide what we are seeking. Yes, there are special risks that come with this opportunity, but let's not forget the opportunities in our apprehension about the risks. I can think of at least seven different directions I have taken in my work as I have sought out what is important to me. I have trained managers, built performance systems, assessed executives, built teams, developed strategies, redesigned work, envisioned futures, and written books all because I wanted to. What I am doing now is miles from what I was doing when I started years ago. That is one of the things I love about being a consultant.

Love of Others

Love has only entered my consulting dictionary within the last five years. (*Sheila Kelly, the Woodlands Group, Roger Harrison, Jack Gibb, and age have profoundly influenced these thoughts.*) I choose to see its entry as an emergence of ancient wisdom rather than a softening of the brain. Now that I am thinking in its terms, I see love all around me when I am working; we just don't call it that, being afraid to acknowledge its presence. I mean, what would it sound like if executives told of a love for each other! Shocking!! So we aren't talking about it much, but we are displaying it a little and (I believe) wanting to show it more. That said, here is a five-word progression, culminating in the "L word."

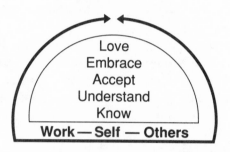

This short, difficult hierarchy is another description of what I am doing in this work and this life. Follow through it with me and notice how it fits and does not fit with your thoughts. I will use the hierarchy to develop a full work relationship with an imaginary client.

First, I need some knowledge of what is happening outside myself. In relation to my work and clients, I collect information about what is going on. In relation to a client, I gather data about his situation. I receive data from him and what surrounds him. The other levels of the hierarchy are dependent on this knowledge. I know the client.

I then seek to understand what is happening, and this is different from knowledge. In talking with a client, I can demonstrate to her that she knows I see her viewpoint. And I have satisfied myself, in putting together the knowledge I have accumulated, that I understand. At this second level, I am trying to absorb the meaning of what is happening to the client. Just listen for how often the word *understand* is used by and around you each day. I know and understand the client.

Acceptance follows understanding. I know and understand the client; I may or may not accept him. To accept him is to receive him, to allow him, to welcome him. To accept the client does not necessarily mean to agree with him. Rather, it means that I see him as a person of value, worth my attention. My acceptance is more important than any particular point that might come up between us. I accept him for who he is; I accept what he says, what he does, what he feels. I see him as a separate and worthwhile person. I know, understand, and accept the client.

Embracing a client's thoughts eliminates distance between us at the acceptance level. This is a hard notion to express; it resembles acceptance but is clearly beyond it. A physical embrace is a good symbol for what I do with the client's thoughts and feelings. I enfold the client's ideas, emotions, issues, and opportunities. I wrap my own thoughts and feelings around hers; I hold what I know of her as important because it is important to her. *And,* I do this apart from whether I agree or disagree with her. So to this point, I know, understand, accept, and embrace the client.

The top level of this hierarchy is love of the client. Though this is related to what can happen in more romantic relationships, I suggest putting romantic love out of mind for a few minutes. How does love work at work? In its ideal expression, distinctions between the client and myself are less important. We are attuned to each other. We open to each other, without fear of each other. Neither of us needs to change to satisfy the other. We each have complete trust that the other will act in ways that serve us both well. There is no need to be protective in any way. And this love builds on knowing, understanding, accepting, and embracing the client.

Later in this book, I explore power and the partnership, emphasizing the importance of creating an equal partnership with our clients, relationships that are open to friendship. As I work with my clients, I am trying to open myself to the love of friends. The authenticity and intimacy created by friends represents a knowable aspiration for me with my client. I am not implying that I must pursue love with every client. I am just demonstrating where the relationship can go and encouraging all of us to be open to that possibility.

Work is such an important part of most of our lives; as consultants we invest a great deal of time in other people. Many of us say we love our work. It seems absurd to me that we should not open ourselves to loving the people we do our work with. As in other loving relationships, there is risk that accompanies growth in the partnership, but ascending this little hierarchy can bring new meaning to work in our lives.

Look for opportunities to care for clients more rather than less. Look into the work they are doing and find what deserves respect, admiration, praise, or honor. See their work from a larger life perspective. See it as a way they have chosen to invest themselves, to find meaning in their lives. Think about, and find out about, what they do outside of work—their hobbies, their families, their community work. All of this will help you build your love for your clients and will help you help them.

If you are having difficulty knowing, understanding, accepting, embracing, and loving this hierarchy of client relationships, know that I had trouble expressing it too. However, it has major consequences for our lives and our work. It is worth reaching for or growing into. It can increase our personal power, our meaning, and our effectiveness. I was tempted to leave it out of this book—to leave it at home with my "loved ones." But that separation is ridiculous and it plays into the workplace's denial of love's presence. I have come to believe in the importance of love of fellow workers as well as love of work. We don't need to establish annual love evaluations. We just need to

Know that it is happening
Understand that it is essential
Accept that it is not easy
Embrace it—if a bit awkwardly
Love the growth of love's expression at work

The Reality

The World Does Not Make Sense

Here is a collection of related statements that are becoming more powerful for me:

- The world does not make sense; we make sense.

- There is not very much around us that we understand in any depth.
- We make constant assumptions about what the world will do as we move through it.
- We really control very little in this world.
- Our reality is of our own creation.

I picture myself as an ice skater, gliding confidently across the frozen surface and unaware of how thin the ice really is, how many cracks are in it, and what lurks in the depths below. That ice is the world as I make sense of it, as I have created it. It holds me to the extent that it makes sense to me. Somehow, I create the ice I skate upon, keeping myself from sinking into the depths. I skate with the assumption that the ice will continue to support me. I skate presumptuously, audaciously, as if I know what I am doing. I create my world and freeze the ice by behaving confidently. I have no alternative but to impose my sense on the world, but it is a great mistake for me to think that the world actually makes my kind of sense. A differently ordered, even chaotic, real world lies beneath the sense I impose on it. It can make sense in so many different ways that it doesn't make any sense at all. Just to acknowledge this is a small threat to my reality. To explore it, to allow this belief to sink in, can seriously threaten me. It is through this view of the world that I consult, trying to help myself and others create meaning.

The Most Important Work Issues Are Life Issues

Through time, I have discovered truth in this for myself—and also for my clients. Our energy for working on a project rises noticeably when we are working on what matters in people's lives, and to the extent that the project can help people

See
Grow
Empower themselves
Find happiness at work
Increase their sense of self-worth
Work together more productively
Discover increased meaning in what they do

To the extent that these things are happening, my clients and I are usually more invested. To the extent that a project is primarily about which product is best, improving systems and procedures, saving money, making money, or getting the plant to run better, I am less invested. I may still do the work: I just do not care as much about it. This is often true for my clients, too.

There is a corollary to this: If my client and I are talking about saving money, developing a product, or plant efficiencies, and we think that this is *the* only point, we are missing the point. We cannot pursue cost efficiencies or product development as ends in themselves. We must be motivated to pursue them because they have something to do with what is important in our lives. Our motivation flows to the extent that we find meaning that goes beyond the savings, the efficiencies—the more immediate demands the business is placing on us. I look for meaning that transcends the immediately obvious. To the extent that I find it and can help others find it, a deeper source of energy is tapped in the organization.

When I play tennis, I don't play as hard as I do because the game of tennis is important. It is just a game, and one that I am not even very good at. I play hard because it allows me to exercise some parts of myself that are important to my self-concept. Concentration, discipline, camaraderie, achievement, power, competition, health, vigor—these are the meaningful parts of myself that I give expression to when I play tennis. And tennis is important only because of all that I gain through it.

When I read a book, I am not doing it to see how fast I can read or how many pages I can read or how many books I can read. I read to allow others to affect my thinking, my imagination. The primary product of my reading is not eighty-seven pages per hour. The primary measure of my tennis game is not the final score. And the primary definition of the health of a corporation is not last quarter's profits. The pages, the score, and the profits are each indicators that deserve attention. It makes no more sense to evaluate a corporation entirely on quarterly profits than it does to evaluate my reading entirely on my pages read per hour.

So my search for meaning in my work goes beyond the numbers that are so readily available. I see them as standing for, representing, something that is more important. I respect the numbers and try to find their place in a larger perspective. I have just as much difficulty with a client who sees the numbers as an end in themselves as I would with a person who brags about how much he or she has read but is unable to tell me what the book was about, or with a tennis player who believes that the final score is all that matters.

I want to help people work on what is important in their lives and particularly on those issues that involve work. This often means helping them gain another perspective on what their life is about so that they can see what work is about.

- For a management team, it may mean figuring out what they would be proud of doing together at their plant, or in their division.
- For a work group, it may mean identifying what professionalism is in their work and what it has to do with what they want out of their lives.
- For an individual executive, it could mean laying out some life goals and deciding what could be done to realize some of those goals over the next twenty years.
- For a client who is entirely focused on the numbers, it means searching for the meaning behind the numbers

We Make a Difference . . .
and It Is Not That Important

I contribute much in this life that is not world-shaping or profound. Oh sure, I have made my small contribution to evolution along with billions of other creatures over millions of years, and it is just not that important. I could stop writing this book, stop working, stop living, and it would not be that important to the cosmos. Yes, I do make a difference—and no, it is not all that important. And it seems that I cannot do very much about the way I see this "reality."

So why bother? Why bother writing? Doing? Being? Because there is some small voice deep inside me that seeks expression, that wants to give meaning to itself, that wants to define itself. It somehow puts aside the relative unimportance of it all and says, "I will become myself." As surely as new leaves form on the plum tree outside my office—without regard for the fact that there will be thousands of leaves on the same tree and on millions of other plum trees around the world—just as surely as that, I am forming, becoming myself. And in the grand scheme of things (if there is a grand scheme), I will mean about as much as one of those plum leaves.

Surprisingly, I find this perspective enlightening, load-lifting, refreshing—even though the place I have found for myself in all of being is not nearly so grand or so exalted as might be desired. I have discussed my views with friends who find my conclusions rather depressing; my world and our roles in it seem hopeless and worthless. I see just the opposite: hope and worth. But the hope and the worth are found in the self, rather than in changing the world. They are found in giving expression to our potential, rather than in some grand importance outside ourselves. The fact that we make a difference in the world around us is obvious as we move through it. We impact people and events. I feel responsible for using myself well to affect what is happening around me. I cannot use my beliefs to excuse myself from making a difference. I can make a small difference and it is vital to me that I do, even though I do not have many illusions about how important those small differences are in the great picture of the universe.

2

Balancing Your Work in Your Life

*T*his chapter focuses on the small actions that tip the larger balance of work and life. Some points seem particularly important if we are to live out our values through our work. For me, many of them center around the amount I work, the amount I travel, and having an office at home. I will discuss each of these topics with the idea that my experiences might help you with your own. I see myself as writing my side of our conversation and you as mentally filling in your side. Notice what ideas our conversation stimulates; notice where we agree and why; notice where we disagree and why. Approaching the chapter in this way fulfills my intention of helping you think about your balance between work and life.

The Work Schedule

How Much Do You Want to Work?

As you will see in the pages that follow, I think that there are some critical decisions to make about when and whether we work. My work decisions affect my life balance profoundly and demonstrate what I value. My decisions and actions are different from those of many of my professional associates. Others tell me that hearing about my approach is useful to them.

If you want to hear stories about how to earn big dollars as a consultant, then buy a consulting book that promises to earn you money. If you want to learn about how one consultant is finding happiness, growth, and value working less than he is "supposed to," then read on.

During eight of my first nine years of consulting, I worked 100 paid days a year. One year I worked about 200 days; that was the year we moved to Seattle and I was establishing myself on the West Coast. I hope I will never do that again. When Sheila, my wife, began working full time, I cut back on my work. For the last five years, I have been working about 80 days a year. My paid days include preparation time; I bill clients for all the time I work for them.

When I add administrative time, the time I give to the community and professional organizations, and the miscellaneous trivia that surrounds the important parts of work, another 30 to 40 days might be added to my work year. I don't know; I have never closely tracked that time.

I do this out of choice, not necessity, and have since I started this business. I estimate that I turn away two to four times as much work as I do. It is hard to know because work possibilities do not come with the total days attached. Since I limit how much work I do, I measure my business more by the amount of work that comes to me than by the amount I actually do. My income increases and decreases in relation to my daily fee, rather than in relation to days worked.

I could do twice as much work and make twice as much money, but I choose not to. I can think of three consultants who work about three times as much as I do. One friend worked 310 days last year, almost four times what I did. The money provokes occasional envy in me, but I don't want to live my life in the way that would allow me to earn it.

I think it is just fine if others want to work more or less than I do, if they are doing what they want to do. As one said to me recently, "You are leading a very balanced life and I am getting rich! We are both doing what we choose and we are both happy."

What do I do with the time that I am not investing in clients? Part of me wants this list to be very impressive, something like:

Play the violin	Climb Mount Rainier
Research	Run ten miles a day
Swim 100 laps	Talk with the mayor
Meditate	

You get the idea. But that is not my list; here is my real list:

Sleep in	Talk with my children
Read books	Write letters
Call friends	Go to lunch with friends
Mow the lawn	Attend conferences
Weed	Drive my wife to work
Fix dinner	Go to movies
Write books	Worry
Run errands	Consider exercising
Listen to music	Take naps
Camp	Go to breakfast with friends
Attend workshops	Work in the community
Clean house	Pay bills

And the pattern that emerges from these individual events suits me well.

I know there are some things on my list that you count as work that I don't, such as going to conferences, attending workshops, or writing books. Yes, some of these activities are good for business, but I don't participate with marketing in mind. I could stop doing all of them and still have plenty of work. I see them primarily as developmental for me. And yes, they do generate some work—less than 10 percent of what I do.

I love this work! I just don't need to do it every day. Work is intentionally a most central part of my life, but I also have many other things to do. When I work too much I don't get to do those other things. I care so much about this work that I would do it even if I were not paid for it. In fact, I *do* it when I am not paid for it.

When I am working, I work hard. No, I don't require a nap in the middle of the day (though that would be nice) and yes, I often work into the night. Like you, I do what must be done, and more, to make my work a success for my client and for me. I often work too much. Three or four times a year, work bunches up on me and I have to do far more in a month than I ordinarily like to do. I know what it is like to work too hard, to be stressed out on a job, to be tired and still be a long way from finished. I don't handle overworking any better than anyone else.

> **One** *consultant's thoughts near the end of*
> **Two** *weeks on the road with*
> **Three** *workshops and*
> **Four** *consultations in*
> **Five** *client systems through*
> **Six** *hotel rooms over*
> **Seven** *thousand miles.*
>
> *I am tired . . .*
> *Tired of being understanding*
> *Tired of listening,*
> *Tired of relating,*
>
> *I am tired of caring, of initiating, of being strong, of being*
>   *my better self.*
> *I want to rest.*
>
> *I know more than I have learned.*

I have experienced more than I have absorbed.
I need to slow down to catch up.

It is someone else's turn.
Someone else's turn
To clarify, to risk, to confront, to support.

It is my turn
to sit back, to care less, to be silent, to coast.

I want to be the rest of me.
I want to be surrounded by softness in light, sound, and
* touch.*
I want pillows and pleasure, comfort, quiet, and calm.

I want it all to come easily. I want friends who ask nothing.
I want a lover to care for me. I want to go home.

(Written between Calgary and Chicago ten years ago.)

While other consultants are flying around the country worrying about whether they are spending enough time with their families, or wearing themselves out through working too hard, I am worrying too. I seldom find consultants who intentionally restrict their work as much as I do. This causes me to "what if":

What if I am being stupid?
What if I am not putting enough aside for my later years?
What if the family has needs I have not planned for?
What if I am playing the grasshopper to everyone else's ant?

I have a pattern of worrying about this; it is one of the things I do in my spare time. I get a little anxious when I think about the money I could make working 100 more days a year. The anxiety is tied to what I know I "should" be doing. Fortunately, while I was writing this my two daughters stopped by my office to visit. We talked just long enough for me to regain perspective.

In case you are still wondering, you do not have to work 280 days a year. The question is, how much do you *want* to work? And, if it is significantly less than you are now working, are you willing to give up what those extra days of work and fees give you for the possible benefits of having those days for yourself?

Some reader is thinking, "Well, hell, yes! Guessing at your level of fees, I could work eighty days a year too!" Keep in mind that I have been doing this for twelve years and it worked when I earned much less per day. The point is that there is a good chance that you could do this too if you wanted to. I am not suggesting that you do it, but that you think about it.

If you are working 40 days a year and wanting to work a *lot* more, 80 probably looks great. And you are in a great position to prepare yourself to work 80. You are being forced to constrain your spending, to think carefully about how you use your resources. The thinking that you are developing during these tougher times will serve you well when you get closer to your goal.

If you are working far in excess of 100 days and have expenses that are supported by all this work and you are happy, then keep at it! Enjoy it! If enjoyment is a more positive word than the one that comes to mind, then consider what you would have to do to limit your work and how that would affect your life.

If you are working on a life strategy that requires you to work hard for many years and save a lot so you can then cut back or even quit, proceed with caution. Though this is a workable strategy—many people have succeeded with it—many others have failed. Here is the part deserving caution: While you are saving a lot and working hard, you are *learning* to save a lot and to work hard. Those learnings are not easily put aside when it comes time to spend savings and work less.

How Effective Can One Person Be?

Let's face it, if you are a one-person organization, there are some projects that you will not have the resources to take on. Further, if you plan to work 80 rather than 240 days a year, your availability is one-third what it might be. This is exactly the combination that I am working with, and it affects my clients. It may cause me to think too much in terms of the projects I am willing to take on, alone, within the time I have available. My parameters limit the resources I make available, which can hamper the project I am working on. In a recent dinner conversation with a client, we were looking down the road at where the project was headed. It was pretty clear to both of us that in about six months, if everything worked out in the interim, a large training effort would be required. I told him that I wanted to help design and perhaps manage that part of the project, but I didn't want to run it myself. It required more work of me than I was comfortable giving to one client. The project, in effect, would have taken most of my work year. I assured the client that when the time came, I would help him find the resources he needed. We agreed to go forward, working within my parameters.

Another alternative available to that client is, "I want a consulting firm that has the resources I need when I need them! This project requires the concentrated efforts of two or three consultants over a three-month period, not the occasional input of a consultant who wants to work part-time!" That is a reasonable alternative; I am fortunate that my client did not see it that way.

My most important concern is the impact of my work parameters on the project. Are the alternatives I offer to the client based primarily on what the project needs? Or do I limit my offered alternatives to those I can provide? These questions occur naturally if you are a one-person firm or a small firm. They occur more often if you are a small firm *and* limit the work you do. I temper my concern about this with the fact that large firms with large resources are faced with their own questions: Are the alternatives we offer based on what the project needs? Do we expand alternatives to create opportunities to use all the resources we have on staff? At the other end of the continuum, they must trouble themselves with whether their clients need all the help they provide.

How Do You Balance All Parts of Your Practice?

This section has to do with the balance within the balance. Your work is balanced with the rest of your life, and within your work different kinds of work receive different amounts of attention. This balance within your work has to do with your growth as a business, as a consultant, and as a person.

It would be too easy to say, "Work is work. If I've got some, that is good enough. What is there to think about?" This kind of thinking disempowers us in the marketplace and the world. It encourages us to see ourselves entirely as a function of other forces. It does not provide room for the influence we can exercise.

Here is a short process that causes me to think about the balance within my work. I suggest that you think through it with me. I will use my work as an example, and you can use your own.

1. We start by looking at the main elements of the work we do. For example, I have four elements to my work: consulting to organizations, counseling executives, training managers, and speaking. These four main elements generate almost all of my income. If you were to divide your work into its three to five main parts, what would those be?

   As you do this, think only about the work you do that actually results in money in your pocket. Put aside for now your administrative work, your marketing and sales work, the non-income-generating work you do in the community, and the conferences you attend. All that is important, too, and must be supported by the core elements of your income-generating work. But before getting to those, it is helpful to see what you are now doing to earn your living.

2. How many days a year do you currently work and how do you currently invest those days to generate income? If the elements in item 1 make up 100 percent of your money-making time, what percentage goes to each? For example, this year I am working about eighty days. Most of that time, a little over sixty days or 80 percent, is going to consulting. About 5 percent is training, another 5 percent is counseling, and about 10 percent is speaking. Do the same rough calculation of where your work goes. Do not guess; go back through your calendar to see where your time really goes. It is easy to fool yourself into thinking you are spending time where you are not.

3. Now that you have a sense of how you are using yourself, it is time to look at how you would like to be using yourself. What would you like the main elements of your paid work to be over each of the next three years? Perhaps there is something that was included in your answer to item 1 that you want to drop, or something you want to add. For example, when I started in this work I was doing training almost to

the exclusion of consultation. And until five years ago I was seldom, if ever, a paid public speaker. So consulting and speaking are examples of main elements I wanted to add to my work a few years ago. There was really nothing I wanted to drop. What are your answers?

4. Now that you have identified the main areas you would like to be working in next year, what percentage of your time would be going to each? Do the same exercise you went through with your present real work, but now build the work mix you would like to have over the next three years. As an example, when I bring all this together, it looks like this.

Main Elements	This Year	Next Year	And Next	And Next
Training	5%	10%	10%	10%
Consulting	80%	60%	65%	70%
Counseling	5%	10%	10%	10%
Speaking	10%	20%	15%	10%
Total Days	80	90	80	70

I will not go into the reasons behind my choices right now, but you can see the direction I would like to move in. At this stage, there is not a lot of dramatic movement for me. That was not the case earlier in my career as a consultant. You may find that your projections from where you are to where you want to be are radically different from mine. One other point: It does not matter if all our projections come out exactly. What is important is for us to think about the balance that we want and to do something to help it come about.

This process causes me to think about what I am doing and really want to do. The thinking that goes into it is more valuable than the numbers that come out. Working through the steps causes me to pay attention. It affects what I really do. Here are some recent examples:

- Yesterday I turned down the opportunity to do over twenty days of management training for an organization because it was simply too much training and too much with one client.

- I am currently talking with another client about doing some executive assessment and development work, because I lost my best counseling client through a merger.

- In my consulting work, my biggest client threatens to overwhelm me with work, so I recently told the managing vice-president that his company had more work than I was prepared to do and that I would help him find another person to do some of it.

- Speaking opportunities seem to just trickle in. If I want to make speaking a larger percentage of what I do, I will have to be more proactive than I am right now.

Think about how your balance, achieved or intended, affects the decisions you make and the actions you take.

How Often Do You Say No to Work?

Many consultants have told me that they seldom, if ever, say no to work. Some were bragging, some were complaining, and they all were quite sure what they would do the next time the phone rang with a potential client on the other end of the line. Why do they almost always say yes and never say no?

"I want to be helpful."
"I can't afford not to."
"When people have problems, I can't turn them away."
"I am flattered that they asked me."
"I don't want to reject them."
"I want them to call me again."
"I don't want them to reject me."
"If I say no today will there be other work tomorrow?"
"I like doing this work so much."
"I don't want to say no to them."
"I simply cannot form the word *N-O* with my lips."

All of these reasons come from successful consultants. Most of these reasons also come from people who talk about being overworked, or stressed out, or out of control, or needing a vacation, family time, or personal time.

When you consider this list in relation to the last one, what possibilities come to mind? My reasoning says that saying no might be a useful way for yes-prone consultants to bring more of what they want into their lives.

I do say no often, and it is not easy for me either. Too often, I say yes at the wrong time. Too often, I find myself caught up in a project that I would rather not be working on. And when I think about it, the clues were there as I began the project. I knew the reasons why I shouldn't do the work then and I ignored them. I said yes when I should have said no. I have done this often enough over the years for some patterns to emerge. If I can identify which work I usually end up wishing I were not doing, then I can say no to it and avoid the discomfort of doing what I really do not want to do. Here is where (it seems) my uncomfortable work comes from; see how my experience fits with your own. (*For further elaboration on this from a different perspective, see "Creating Frustration and Failure" in Chapter Ten.*)

Small projects.   When I find myself regretting having taken on work, it is usually a small- to medium-sized project—one to five days of work. I can recall few major projects that I wished I could magically remove myself from. I suspect that I do a better job of checking out and contracting on large projects.

Time-consuming projects.   Tied to the first point, the small piece of work ends up taking much more time than I expected it would take—and more time than it should take. Getting paid for this time is small solace because all through the project I know that "this shouldn't be taking this much time!" I often can't bring myself to charge the client for the extra time because the cost would be exorbitant for the product delivered. So I eat it, causing myself additional exasperation in the process.

Local work.   Most of my troubling work has been local. It is easier for me to say no to potential clients from outside my own area. I am more conscious of my reputation at home than around the country. Having practiced here for nine years, I am known by more people. I imagine that clients and potential clients talk with each other about using me. I want them to say good things; I don't want them to say that I turned down their request to work for them. So in order to maintain the sterling reputation I hold in my consultant fantasies, I take on work that

I don't really want to do and will probably not do very well. Dumb, but true!

Work for friends.   It is difficult for me to say no to friends—or even friends of friends. I am easily seduced into agreeing to work for them. I have taken on projects that I didn't want to do that really could have been done better by someone else. I have agreed to speak on subjects that are outside my expertise and interest and required far too much research to get ready. I have done this so people would continue to like me and say nice things about me. I know, it doesn't make sense, but that is what I have done—and continue to do.

Certain types of clients.   This is a shaky point for me; I am not sure of it yet. Patterns seem to be emerging in relation to the kinds of clients I work well with and do not work as well with. For example, I have worked with three clients in the health care industry in the last five years. Although the results of our work together ranged from satisfactory to terrific, my feelings about the work are laced with discomfort. I am beginning to believe that health care is not a setting I work well in. I believe this so much that earlier this week when a hospital called inquiring about my interest in running a management retreat, I declined and recommended someone else.

Certain levels of clients.   Within client organizations, which levels do you work best with? Do you have any patterns of *not* working well with a particular level? I seem to work better at management levels and can see some pattern of my not dealing as well with hourly workers. This is not a matter of preference, but a matter of effectiveness, and it gives me clues about work I could say no to.

This is what I have been able to figure out so far. Think back over the work you have done that you wish you had said no to. What patterns emerge for you?

If You Cannot Say No, Can You Really Say Yes?

This is an important question. If you accept every piece of work that comes in your direction for five years, are you really choosing? There is the appearance of choice, but when the answer is always the same, do you have any choice? Think about it.

I learned this perspective from a friend who was having problems in her relationships with the opposite sex, problems reminiscent of Ado Annie's refrain in *Oklahoma:* "I'm Just a Girl Who Can't Say No." My friend's therapist asked her, "If you cannot say no, can you really say yes?" The impact of this question and its answer was profound for her. She saw the choices she had given away, the ways in which she had disempowered herself and contributed to her own unhappiness. Understanding that, she could now behave differently. And she did.

The parallel with our work is clear. What can we do to avoid being consultants who can't say no?

The Travel Schedule

How Long Does It Take to Get to Work?

How far do you want to travel to work? To your office? Would you travel across town? Across the country? Across the world? Could you travel if you wanted to? Will your home situation support it? Will your work allow it?

Travel presents serious questions. It is so grueling that you have to choose it to make it bearable. Choosing it does not make it easy; it just puts it within the realm of choice rather than obligation. It has a major impact on your life and your energy. One day of work on the other side of the country takes at least two full days with travel, not to mention changing time zones. A day of work near home is just that.

I intentionally travel to do my work for many reasons:

- I don't think the client base where I live is large enough to support me in the diversity of work I want to pursue.
- I run the risk of being seen narrowly by my present and future local clients. My reputation is likely to build from a narrower base and I will be seen as a narrower consultant.
- Other markets support higher fees than the local market. This reason is not as compelling as some of the

others. I know that if the fees were the same, I would still work in other parts of the country.

- I like the recognition that comes with being the expert from out of town; I think my clients like it too. I also think my local clients like to hire a consultant whom others are willing to fly across the country.
- Travel defines me as a national consultant; this is one distinguishing element when clients are trying to figure out who I am and what I do.

One year after moving to Seattle, I was caught in the traffic in Houston, Texas, creeping toward (apparently) the same destination everyone else on the road wanted to reach. It dawned on me, "I didn't move to Seattle to be tied up in traffic in Houston!" At the time I was not doing any work in Seattle; I decided then and there to change that. (*See "Writing as a Marketing Tool" in Chapter Thirteen for a description of how I made this change.*)

Over the last five years I have been working about a quarter of my work days close enough to home so that I can be home in the evening. This balance is not easy to maintain; it seesaws radically as projects come and go. But it is clear that paying attention to this balance has made a difference.

Your consulting reputation will build locally—whether you do anything about it or not. If you are doing any work around your city, people will talk about you. And they will probably talk about you with people from other organizations who are potential clients. Over a five-year period, you will see the number of calls you are getting from close-to-home potential clients increasing—as long as your clients have been saying good things about your work. Said another way, the need for local marketing is less because your client base is geographically concentrated and will do your most important marketing work for you.

Look at the size of your local market: Can it support you long-term? Does it make sense to expect that a significant amount of your business will come from the local market over the long term? Can you build a life and practice working with local clients? Will they be as anxious to see you twenty years from now as they are today? (For someone just starting out who doesn't have any business, this can seem like a ridiculous consideration. Put it aside for now and come back to it in a few years.)

With work, related meetings, and conferences, I am away from home an average of eight nights a month. I am seldom gone weekends and when I am, it is usually not to work. I do find myself getting on planes on Sunday evening, cutting a chunk off the end of my family time. All in all, the schedule is tolerable; it only gets to me about three times a year, when I have managed it poorly and overcommitted myself.

The positive side of my travel schedule is that when I am home, I am home! In fact, I am home now much more than I was in my last two positions in industry. There, I traveled a significant amount and when I was not traveling, I was away from home ten to twelve hours a day. Now I am home more often to do whatever I want and the family wants.

An up side of travel is all that uninterrupted time on airplanes that is available to do what you like. I routinely schedule work and play into my high-altitude time. Since I know what a pain travel can be, I plan to use that time enjoyably and productively.

Where You Live and Where You Work

One way to avoid travel for work (and perhaps for vacations) is careful choice of where you live. Consulting has allowed me to choose where I live. That latitude comes with consulting success; working in corporations does not provide this same choice. To do my work, I need a telephone within reach and an airport within easy driving distance. There are thousands of places in this country that meet these two criteria. For two summers I worked out of a phone booth on an island with occasional plane service. On a temporary basis that was just fine.

Living where you want to live means that each day at home you have something extra to celebrate. You can pause to enjoy your home and what surrounds you, knowing that is where you choose to be. A commitment to a place allows you to put down deeper roots, to invest yourself more fully than you might imagine. This can have a profound impact on your life and well-being, which is reflected in your work. Deciding where you want to live is one of the more important decisions external consulting allows and even encourages you to consider. You may not be able to act on the choice immediately, but you can begin to plan for the day you will move.

The Office

Working at Home

Do you need to get away from home in order to work?

Does wearing business attire help you work better?

Do you need an office you can invite clients to?

Do you need daily personal contact with grown people who do work related to your own?

Do you value the status of having an office in a real office building?

If you answer a resounding *yes!* to two or more of those questions, then this section is probably not for you. And those readers who have decided absolutely that they will not have an office at home might as well skip this section too.

For those of you who are still with me, listen to this:

"Could I use your markers?"

"Would you kids please stop yelling when I am on the phone!"

"Where is my stapler?"

"Dinner's ready!"

"Could you give me a ride to work?"

"Would you kids please clean up the toys in my office?"

"Who spilled cocoa on my computer?"

Or . . .

You are in the middle of an important telephone conversation with a client, but your daughter wants to know whether she can stay overnight with a friend—and she wants to know *now!*

Or . . .

You have a report to finish before Federal Express picks up, and the garbage is overflowing, and there isn't a clean towel in the house, and the cat just threw up on the rug.

All of the above is part of why I have my office in my home. There is no escaping it; you are at home—and you are at work. Both are true much of the time. For me, all of this creates perspective and balance. The daughter, the report, the cat, the garbage, and the laundry are all part of life. And I find that life richer for having them in close proximity rather than antiseptically distant. One of the reasons I have my office at home is so that I can face these real and conflicting priorities.

Here is an opportunity to balance our lives, and to gain that balance not by separating work and home but by putting them together. To have one part of your mind absorbing a client's problem and another part absorbing a child's problem—that's perspective! At least it is the opportunity for perspective; or it can just be maddening. You will decide how you will deal with it. As long as you have your office at home and other people or animals around, you will have "opportunities" like this.

Thirteen years ago I started working out of my home out of necessity; now it is out of choice. Since there is no real separation of home and office, I have to manage the interface of the two. With practice, it has become much more a pleasure than a pain. What are its pleasures?

- My family knows more about my work because they see me work.
- I know more about the family because I am here a great deal of the time.
- I am available if needed to help with homework, to talk, to fix dinner, or for an emergency.
- I can come and go from work easily.
- My family likes me better because they know me better.
- Family life puts work in perspective. It gives me a better sense of how important (or unimportant) my various projects are.
- How many professionals in this world can go to work in their pajamas, do work they love, make money, and not worry about being arrested? It is so comfortable to be able to go to the office without going through a morning grooming and dressing ritual.

And the pains of working at home?

- Family members (especially children) do not always respect the importance of your work to you.
- If you plan on expanding your business, adding more people or huge inventories is difficult to do at home.

- It can be very tiring to work all day on a report and also prepare meals and take care of other family needs.
- When your children are young and you are the only adult at home, it is almost impossible to maintain a span of attention and keep track of the kids.
- The rest of the family becomes very familiar with "your" work space—as when your children discover that your office is a great place for a slumber party.
- There are conflicts in the use of office equipment, for instance, when a daughter has a paper due and you have a report due the next morning—and you were both planning to use the one computer!

Even as I am writing about these "pains," I am saying to myself that they are not so bad. We manage them. And we all understand and appreciate each other much more.

I just took a short break from writing to go into the house and get a cup of coffee. My office is connected to the house, but I have to go outside to get from one to the other. I noticed a new weed taking over a corner of the lawn. I stopped, pulled a few, then a few more. Twenty minutes later I finished, got my coffee, and am back at the keyboard to write. This is a good example of what happens when you work at home. I have come to expect interruptions—either of my own making or by others. And the result is perspective.

What helps home offices work?

- Try to have separate physical work space with walls, or a screen, or an electric fence around it.
- Locate that space upstairs from, around the corner from, in the next room from, or down the hall from other parts of your life. It also ought to be a little out of the way, so that other people don't pass by frequently. Do not place yourself off a busy hallway or in the family room.
- Have a business telephone that can only be answered in your office; if possible, don't have a home telephone in the office.

- Keep all of your work stuff in that space. Do not begin to adapt the house into your office because other people will not respect it. You will not find files, books, checks, or anything else you leave around.
- Quiet, fresh air, and good light are pleasant for you to work in.
- Have a clear understanding with the rest of the people you live with about whose space this is, how you want it treated, and how you want to work. With smaller children, rules are good reminders.
- If you put your office in your bedroom, you will work twenty-four hours a day. If you put your office in your kitchen, you will live on snacks and frozen dinners. If you put your office in your living room, you will have friends over less often. There is such a thing as having work too close to your home life, and you run that risk when you work at home.

For those of you who are currently officed outside your home, I hope you found some of these opportunities tempting. All of you who are currently working at home know that it can work.

Administrivia

(*This section is dedicated to Forrest Belcher, a friend and associate who saves everything!*) I don't have many words about how to make your office work, but I could not resist contributing my thoughts about how to keep it small and manageable. So for the next few pages I will focus on (ugh!) files. I believe that files are a living thing, like a garden, that can become a jungle. Like most gardens, they need regular weeding and pruning. Since files are self-fertilizing, they need extra attention from you or they will gradually take over your entire office. Those of you more inclined to continue adding file drawers might want to skip this section.

Rule 1. Never buy paper clips. In a dozen years of doing this work, I have never purchased a box of paper clips. I started off with a small, half-full box that somehow made it home with me when I moved out of the last company I worked for. I now have a cigar box that is full of paper clips and clamps.

All of these clips and clamps have been sent to me. I am receiving more than I am sending out; therefore, I am successful! One of my purposes in this life is *not* to cover my clients with paper; my clip inventory gives me some small indication that I am succeeding. If I had to buy paper clips on a regular basis, I would have left this work long ago. The number of clips in my collection tells me something about my files, which leads to . . .

Rule 2. Prune your client files at least annually. That pile of clips comes from all the paper that has moved across my desk. Some of it goes into my files. The rest of it is "de-clipped" and de-stroyed. Each paper clip in that cigar box represents paper that is not in my files. And clamps represent pounds of paper that are not in my files. I try (and usually succeed) to keep all of my active client files in one drawer. When the drawer gets too tight, I go through it and prune the departed clients. Clients that are no longer mine and the paper in their files shouldn't be in the active drawer. I have always succeeded in creating the room I need in my client drawer.

What happens to the old client files? They are stripped down to the legal essentials that the IRS might be interested in and placed in a box in a storage closet. When that gets too full (you guessed it) the box is pruned out, with records from seven-plus years ago getting the heave-ho.

Rule 3. Prune your resource files quarterly. By "resource files" I mean all those articles, models, handouts, pamphlets, and booklets you save in case you might ever need them. I keep them alphabetized by subject area in four file drawers. Associates, clients, and friends conspire to send me stacks of this useful stuff. Their unspoken intent is that I be found one day, dead, under a stack of "leading edge" articles that fell on me while I was feeding the mice that make their home in these piles of erudite, thought-provoking, stimulating trash! But, knowing their evil intent, I am hard at work against them. I am determined not to fill my office with all this impressive pulp. I will not be opening a mouse haven. I will not have the life pressed out of me by a collapsed tower of *Harvard Business Review*s!

To avoid this fate, I stack the materials as they arrive (there is a three-foot-high stack waiting for me right now). I go through a whole stack at one sitting, physically tearing journals apart, sorting out everything that I might want to read, scan, or save, and throwing away everything else—which is about 80 to 90 percent of what I receive. All that potentially good reading goes in a stack and a part of that stack goes with me on each trip I take, where it is read and saved or rejected. This leaves a much smaller stack of articles that are destined for my resource files, which are in the four file drawers already brimming over with consulting wisdom.

How do I get this new short stack of irreplaceable brilliance into these four drawers? More pruning. I go through the alphabetized files looking for a content area that used to be essential knowledge but that is now volunteering to offer its space (and life) to new essential knowledge. Let's see . . . "Excellence." That looks like a content area that could stand a little pruning. So the three inches of excellence materials gets pruned to a fourth that size. And so on, until there is enough room for all the new files. This isn't as difficult (at least for me) as you might imagine. And when you consider the alternative of saving everything and taking it to your grave with you (most likely a premature grave when this stuff falls on you), you may find the pruning to be a good idea.

The articles that are pruned quarterly do not necessarily disappear from use. They can be recycled to other consultants or professional societies, who will like you for being so nice to them. Maybe you could send some of the mice along with the articles.

Rule 4. Do with your books what you did with your files. (I am aware that I am moving into sacred territory for some of you.) No, don't take them apart at the bindings. But do not add indefinitely to your bookshelves either. I am not suggesting that you quit reading, just that you do not have to own everything you read. When your shelves fill, use the same kind of thinking on your books that you used on your resource files. It is just short of a sin to throw away a book, so make sure that someone else has the opportunity to use your less-used books.

One of the things you learn when going through your shelves looking for space is how much you have grown. You really have learned a lot over the last few years! When you see a book you used to be fascinated with that no longer holds much interest, you know that something in you has changed. And you will find that there are some books that make the cut every time because you continue to turn to them as a resource. The book you are holding is no doubt one of those books!

Rule 5.   There was a rule 5 but I pruned it. Four balance rules are enough.

PART

Two

OPENING THE ORGANIZATION

*T*his part of the book is about doing the work and producing the results that justify our unique role in client organizations. It is about opening the organization to the future, helping it move beyond the present.

As critical as it might be to us to have our work contribute meaning to our lives, as important as it is to build and maintain a powerful partnership with our clients, as essential as money and marketing are to our survival, they all depend on our success in opening the organization to change.

Part Two concentrates on the work we do in organizations, rather than the relationships we build with clients, if I can make that temporary distinction. The next part, "Power and the Partnership," elaborates on how we develop lasting relationships with clients while we do our work. Sorting the work from the relationship is artificial, but it is less confusing to write about them separately, and it may be more useful to read in two parts.

I see four main "players" in this work-accomplishment dynamic. It starts with people in the organization becoming aware of some difference between what they have (Present: "is") and what they would like to have (Future: "want"). They want a change, large or small. This awareness combines with a belief that they could use help from outside to move from where they are to where they want to be. Enter the consultant, bringing

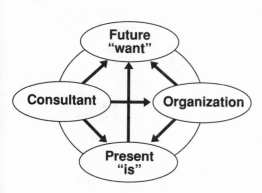

experience and perspective to put beside the organization's experience and perspective. Combining what the organization and the consultant know usually results in some new action and often a change toward what the organization wants or needs or both. Here is how this four-way dynamic affects the content of "Opening the Organization":

- First, I will share my views on how a consultant best consults, including how active, visible, and important we should be as we work in organizations (upper left on the model).

- Then we will consider the organization and how it works—or at least one way of looking at it (lower right on the model).

- This is followed by a brief description of the work dynamic between the consultant and the organization (the diagonal line between the consultant and the organization).

- We will end with a collection of ideas for opening the organization and bringing about positive change. These ideas move from a present toward a future orientation (the diagonal line between Present: "is" and Future: "want").

3

The Consultant
as Leader

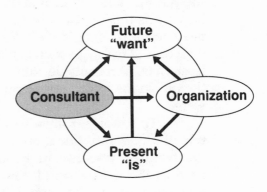

Facilitating Is Not Enough

*T*welve years ago I saw myself as a kind of organizational lubricant. I was an enabler, a helper working with clients to free up rusty parts, a kind of "WD-40" that allowed the industrial gears to turn more quickly, quietly, and in relation to each other. Whatever the organization's purpose, I was there to see to it that it did what it did better, faster, and more effectively. Though that role is still part of what I do, something has changed.

In those days, these comments were typical of what you would hear from me, the facilitator, in groups:

"John, I am noticing that as you talk, you maintain eye contact with Phil and seldom look at others in the group."

"Gertrude, if you were to rephrase your question and make it a statement, what would it be?"

"I hear that you are about to make a group decision, and I am aware that over half of you have not spoken up during the discussion."

These often useful comments brought information to the group that they were unaware of and included no direct statement from me, the facilitator. I saw my role as helping them become aware of what was happening through my observations. That role was and is useful. More was possible.

From the beginning, something was missing for me in this role. As helpful as the role might have been in keeping the wheels turning, it did not include asking questions about whether the wheels ought to turn at all, or whether these are the particular wheels that ought to be turning, or whether this many wheels need to be turning, or whether they need to be turning in this direction. These questions were outside my facilitator's role—at least they were outside the way I had learned the role. And if the questions were outside my role, then their answers certainly were.

This was a role whose substance was form. It was the role of an organizational butler or maid, written in to assure that the featured players could move through their lines smoothly, so that the drama could come off without a hitch. Offstage I wondered about the role; I knew I had more to contribute. I confirmed this through discussion with others. On stage, I began to improvise, stretching the boundaries of the facilitator role. I began to offer ideas on the content that was being discussed in meetings. I encouraged others to share in the facilitator role, to rely less on me. I tested my altered role on people; I asked for support from them for this new role. All that went very well. My excitement with my work increased with the growth in the role. I was being encouraged to speak up on the substance, not just the form, of work. I was asked to lead meetings, rather than just facilitate them.

This resulted in my seeing myself as a leader rather than a facilitator. I now see myself as one leader among the many in the room and I exercise my leadership as legitimately as others exercise theirs. How does this affect what I do?

- I am clear that I am not here just to help the client with his or her agenda. I develop my own agenda and pursue it openly. I respect their agenda and will yield to it; it is their organization, not mine.
- I reach beyond process interventions; I deal in content. I recognize that I have less knowledge about the content of their work; I respect the knowledge and experience they bring.
- When I believe I understand their content, and I have an important opinion, I offer it. My silence on issues is not because speaking up is inappropriate to my role.
- I frequently lead major parts of meetings. I provide the structure we work within directed toward outcomes we all support. I push, pull, tease, test, pontificate, praise, and joke with the group as I help us produce.
- I offer substantive alternatives to clients that go beyond what they have developed on their own.
- I develop beliefs on what ought to be done. I recommend action to the client group.
- I begin to think and act as if I am a part of this organization. I try to behave in the owner's best interests.

Notice that these content interventions do not tell the client how to make steel, produce oil, fly airplanes, or coat candy. I participate less in those technical core functions, except to ask questions and understand. The content I do wade into is usually related to the changes they—we—are trying to bring about. You might hear me say things such as, "I've listened to what everyone has said and here is what I think you ought to do . . ." Or "I think what this group wants to do is . . ." Or even "I think you people are about to make a bad decision. It's your company, but this decision would hurt the company by . . ." I see these three examples as content interventions. A content-plus-process intervention would be, "What have we been doing for the last thirty minutes? I don't think you are ready to make this decision." Or "I think Herb is making a good point and that the rest of you are not hearing what he is saying."

The results for me and my clients are much better than when I performed my more confined facilitator role. I know I am bringing more of my abilities to bear on the clients' issues. The clients see more of my influence on their actions and derive more value from my presence.

It is no longer effective enough for me just to comment on how the clients are doing what they are doing. Comments on how they are approaching work differ from comments that question whether this is the work that should be done. Interventions focused on providing clear structure for clients to reach their goals differ from interventions in which their goals are questioned.

Broadening our role, intervening in content, moves us into a leadership position with our clients. Leading our clients requires vision, strategic intention, risk taking, patience, persistence, and an investment that goes beyond what is expected of us as facilitators. We will be asked to invest ourselves over the long term in ways that run parallel to our clients' own investment.

None of this guidance assumes that we are the only leaders. None of it assumes that we will lead all of the time. We will frequently follow others, usually the same people we will lead at other times. They will be leading most of the time, since we have chosen to be consultants to the organization rather than the full-time manager/leader of it. In suggesting that we can lead as well as facilitate, I know that I am introducing potential problems. The power dynamic with our clients shifts; balance is harder to maintain as we complicate what was a useful observer role with the reality of being a player.

Becoming the Consultant-Leader

*Y*ou may want to lead if:

- You hold strong beliefs and values about your work.
- You envision more ideal ways of working, toward which you think the work world ought to move.
- You frequently have strong opinions about what your clients ought to do next.
- You want to have a profound influence on your client organizations.
- You are action oriented.

As I see it, positive responses to all of these statements make leadership compelling. In fact, *not* to lead would be frustrating. I see leaders as people with clear vision and values who act to bring their dreams to realization, building on the motivation and commitment of others, and who have the patience to persist. I see nothing in that description that precludes consultants from applying. Following is some other support for the consultant-leader:

- I see pure facilitation as a following role. In its strictest form, the facilitator comments on the action without being part of the action, going where the action goes, or offering observations in a play-by-play description. It is a very useful contribution to most groups—and it does not take care of my life needs.
- I realize that I am invested in getting something done in this life through my work—something that goes beyond helping others do what they want to do.
- Because work is a central part of my life, I cannot easily distinguish between my personal and professional selves; my personal and professional beliefs are inseparable. I have certain underlying beliefs that cause me to lead.
- I believe in the underlying dignity of humankind and pursue this dignity for myself, my family, my friends, client organizations, and our society. (*I am grateful to Marvin Weisbord for bringing the word "dignity" to me*

through his book, Productive Workplaces: Organizing and Managing for Dignity, Meaning, and Community.)

- I want to help create work environments in which people can respect themselves for what they do and how they do it. I want individuals' self-esteem to increase through the nature of the work they do and their contacts with other people. There are constant opportunities to intervene on behalf of human growth; I want to use those opportunities to lead my clients in directions they might not have chosen if I had not been there.

- I want to become more fully myself. I want to give expression to what is important to me, to my thoughts, my actions, my feelings. I want to push out the edges of who I am, experience myself more fully.

- I want to influence what happens around me; I want to make a difference. As insignificant as that difference might be when looked at from a cosmic perspective, it is all that I can do. Part of making a difference at work is acting on my beliefs.

- I want to act on my values and do not want to withhold them when working with clients. I want to contribute my thoughts and feelings. I want to serve this small community and the larger community it serves.

Reading about my beliefs will give you a sense of why leading is sometimes compelling to me. Understand that in making my personal statement I respect others' beliefs. I am acting on my beliefs; I expect them to act on theirs. This is essential to my notion of progress. I see leadership as a shared opportunity and count myself as one who is willing to use that opportunity.

4

Understanding How Organizations Work

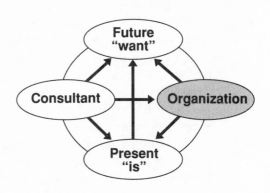

What We Don't Know About Organizations

"*I*n the beginning was General Motors . . ." is *not* the way the Old Testament begins. The organizations we work for are very recent in world history. Stretch out one arm—the one that is not holding this book. (Yes, really. Even if you are on the bus. I want to make a point.) Imagine that your outstretched arm represents time. Your shoulder is the beginning of human life on Earth, stretching out to the present, at the end of your pointing index finger. Companies (and consultants) came into being somewhere near the end of your fingernail. That gives some perspective on how important large organizations have been over time. They are a relatively recent phenomenon and there is still a great deal we do not know about how they work. What we accept as givens in organizational life should be anything but that. We simply cannot explain much of what happens in our organizations; we don't know enough about them yet.

Clients hire consultants because they think we understand organizations. Perhaps you do understand; I know that I do not. I make my living mainly by proclaiming what I don't understand and then seeking further understanding. That is what interviews, listening, empathy, and data collection are all about—reaching further understanding of what is happening in an organization.

Organizations are large, awkward, and unwieldy. People put them together so that other people could pool their talents to produce goods and services. Usually organizations don't work very well because they don't fit the human creatures who work in them. We struggle to help—to make—organizations work; we have no choice but to continue that struggle if we want to keep living in the world we have built around ourselves. But we would do well to question the structures people are laboring within. There must be alternatives that use people's talents better, meet people's life needs better, while delivering the products and services the world needs.

Organizations as we have built them are more mechanical than "organical." We have lost the "organ" in *organization* as we have built awkward hierarchical structures with boxes and lines connecting them. Consider the sister words to *organization*, such as *organ*, *organism*, and *organic* (not to mention *orgasm* and *orgy*);

these words are filled with life! Instead of creating rich, life-filled, working organisms, too often we have created structures modeled after machines—mechanistic, sharply defined, and inflexible—that force their moving human parts to act like machines too. The structures we have created usually do not serve the needs of the people who make them run. These structures should be in service to their entire work force, their community, their vendors, their marketplace, and the environment, not just to their customers and the stockholders. Our challenge is to find ways of creating organizations that will better serve all the people invested in them.

Organizations Do Not Work

*Y*ears ago I was leading a consulting skills workshop in which we had just spent about thirty minutes hearing various participants talk about problems in their respective organizations. We had used almost every reason in the list to complain. I interrupted our moaning to ask, "Who here works for an organization that is basically pretty screwed up?" Together, about 80 percent of the people in the room raised their hands. There was a silent pause—and then we all began to laugh! The message was clear: It is screwed up almost everywhere! Understanding that provides great relief and release.

To elaborate: In this imperfect world full of imperfect people, we try to get things done through large, imperfect organizations—organizations of our own creation. These organizations attempt to bring together a complex combination of resources to meet a wide array of often conflicting needs. Such organizations do not work very well. Even when everyone and everything is finely attuned to what the organization is about, there are significant difficulties. Where is it written that a twelve-tiered organization of ten thousand people across fifty states and twenty product lines should be without strife? Or even a three-tiered structure of fifty people, all in one room, delivering the same service?

The assumptions underlying our discomforts with organizations are often downright laughable. It's as if we really expect them to work! And we are astonished when they do not. What is truly astonishing is that we get so much done through these awkward systems and structures. That reality is a great testimony to the human spirit and the need to find meaning in our lives.

So it is easy to find out what's wrong and more difficult to find out what's right. We routinely hear ourselves and others talk about what a hard week we are having, or the killer meeting this morning, or how unreasonable management is, or . . . The list goes on and on. Granted, it *is* a hard week, the meeting *was* tough, and so is the boss. But why do we keep talking about it? The organization continues to serve up opportunities for us to talk about what's screwed up, broken, not working, and stupid.

We operate as though perfect performance is normal and all else is the exception and deserves to be complained about. Think about the assumptions behind the pattern of griping you hear in an organization. My bet is that most of the time the unspoken assumption is, "This place should be perfect." But organizations don't work. We need assumptions that support a human level of performance.

Organizations Do Not Make Sense

*W*e talk as if what we do in our lives makes sense, as if we do what we do because we are reasonable. I used to believe that; I don't believe it any longer. Oh, certainly there are many actions I take each day that make sense; that's why I do them. And most of them (all of them?) are not very important. For something to be important in my life, I must be invested beyond the sensible, rational level. More of my total person must be present. My head decides whether to get my car serviced today, or what time to call a client, or how many pages of this book I will write, but none of those decisions is very important. I can let my head take care of them. When it comes to deciding whether to be a consultant, where to live, or whether to have a family, the decisions are too big for my head to handle alone. I must reach beyond my rational faculties for guidance.

Consider the big decisions you have made in your life. How many of them were purely rational? My wife and I talked about our big decisions of the last twenty-eight years and we could not find one that was primarily rational. Getting married, having children, working and living where we lived, going to graduate school, becoming a consultant, moving to Seattle—none of these decisions drew primarily on our rational faculties. Certainly we had a rationale for each decision but that usually came after the decision. Test our experience against your own.

If there is some truth in this for you and others, and if those others work in large organizations, then I imagine that important organizational decisions are not made because they are logical and rational. Logic and rationality are used in support of decisions, as a kind of psychic insurance. Every day you can see people on television or in the press explaining why they did what they did. Often in listening you can tell (or think you can tell) that this is their rationalization for doing what they wanted to do. I hope they are not fooling themselves in the process.

There is so much in organizations that does not make sense; let's quit pretending that it *all* makes sense. The chances are that you spent a good part of today wearing a necktie or pantyhose or both. Now that doesn't make sense! What you are paid doesn't make sense! Sure, you have a rationalization for it, but there is nothing objectively rational about your reasoning. Organizations swing through cycles of centralization and decentralization, and they don't do it because it makes sense. CEOs select executives who are first of all loyal and only secondarily have managerial competence. That doesn't make sense! Executive offices are far larger than they need to be to conduct business. Doesn't make sense! Much of business and life does not make sense, and I am not arguing that it should. Instead I am arguing against pretending that it should. Let's accept the idea that much of what we call rational is really rationalization. It's the logical excuses we make for doing what we really want to do—or for doing what someone else wants us to do.

Accept the "Non-Sense"

It makes sense to remember that organizations do not make sense. One of the best ways to make yourself sick is to expect organizations to be rational. Expect them to make sense, demand that they be logical, require that they be reasonable—and expect to have ulcers. Accept that this is the CEO's pet project and that is the reason it is being pursued, regardless of what the press releases say. Accept the reality that the vice-president of sales just flat doesn't like the comptroller and that the reasons they give for not working together are a ruse. Accept this production team's fear of bringing forth new ideas and accept that engineer's zealous pursuit of her project goals. These behaviors go beyond the rational. Logic would dictate that a different path be taken.

The up side of this irrational investment is that people can bring more informed energy and focus than reason could ever demand. This is the motivation managers are so often seeking. The down side is that people can use their less rational selves to restrict their energies, to misdirect or twist the ways they invest themselves. There is no way of accepting the up side and rejecting the down side; they are two sides of the same phenomenon. What differences do exist are in our perception. When people are doing what we want them to be doing, we see that as positive and its opposite as negative. Truly exceptional organizational behavior depends on the right kind of irrationality.

Are you running around client organizations muttering, "This doesn't make sense!" Or "They are so unreasonable!" Or "Logically, they ought to . . ."? If you have a pattern of behaving in these "rational" ways and it is accompanied by headaches, chest pains, stomach pains, or constipation, then maybe it is time for you to take a look at your expectations of your clients. Demanding that people be reasonable and logical is a tremendous drain on you, especially if the demands are not being met. Accepting clients as they are is a different path from imposing order on them. The more accepting path is rich with mystery, intrigue, passion, confusion, and out-and-out craziness, and it is the way people are. Taking it means loosening your hold on rationality and (perhaps more threatening) releasing the reins of control. When you accept that people will behave in ways that don't make sense to you, you have opened yourself to an overwhelming array of options, an array that goes far beyond what the rational can offer.

I see reason as a guide, not a dictator. It is one of a number of guides, all offering their services to us. Intuition is also a guide. So is emotion. In organizations, reason is too often the only acknowledged guide. Emotionally based insight is forced to enter under the guise of reason, rather than being accepted for what it is. We can assist our clients in understanding the guides they are following. We can help them explore what is reasonable and logical, and how that is related to their emotional investment in the situation. We can help them legitimize both "This is what makes sense . . ." and "This is what we want . . ." We can help them do what they want to do without pretending that it makes sense. And we can help them avoid doing something that makes sense that they don't want to do.

Organizations . . . Change . . . Slowly

*D*espite years of experience with helping large organizations change, I still routinely help organizations *under*estimate what it takes to create change. I help them over-simplify what can be done and how it can be accomplished. My best guesses usually fall far short of what is actually required in time, energy, and dollars to bring major change about. And my estimates are far larger than the ones my clients usually come up with. What I think will require three years, they think might take a year. We all have a lot to learn.

One of the main reasons efforts to change large systems falter is because most people did not know what they were signing up for when they began. We have to learn more about what really happens when we try to change an organization. We must let go of our naïve assumptions and our need for immediate action.

One of my favorite client companies is in the middle of a total corporate restructuring. I am an observer and occasional helper in this process. Thousands of lives are being affected, hundreds of families are relocating, others will retire, and thousands of jobs are changing. I am sure that the amount of energy expended on this effort far exceeds what management anticipated when they started this major change. It will be six to eight years before this organization returns to a balance similar to the one it had before all this began. This is not an argument against their restructuring; in fact, I support it. But there must be very compelling reasons for a change of this magnitude to justify such a consuming effort. We need to help our clients understand the immensity of their undertakings before they commit to them.

Do not read this as an argument against change in organizations. Quite the opposite—it is an argument for knowing the truth about change. A change with a large time and resource perspective will probably help people accept the inevitable obstacles as givens rather than as tests of will and patience.

We Arrived Here with Intention

*C*onsider any company you have worked with. Many people worked very hard to bring this company to where it is today. This organization reached this point because of the intentions of hundreds or thousands of people through its history. Whatever shape it is in right now is because of the hard work of these people. This is not to say that all those people wanted the company to be where it is today. No, but they worked hard—as hard as you and I work—and that deserves to be respected. Respect the energy, the intelligence, the sweat, the motivation, the spirit, and the intention that has gone into bringing the organization to this point. And yes, respect the well-intentioned mistakes, the misguided failures, the human foibles, the ulcers, and the tears that are part of where the organization is now. For better or for worse, many people have worked very hard to bring the organization to this moment.

The future is built upon the past. The chances are that the resources that move the organization forward will be largely drawn from the same resources that brought it to where it is today. Maybe the resources will be supplemented, maybe they will be used differently, but most of what is needed to move the organization forward is in the organization right now. Our challenge is to help our clients to find it, uncover it, transform it, align it, or even create it out of what we find.

What can we do and what should we not do?

- Our risk as consultants is acting as if nothing worthwhile happened before our arrival on the scene. We risk showing disrespect for all that these people have spent years laboring to create. Whether it is beautiful or ugly, it is theirs, and they are invested in it.
- When we suggest that there may be some big changes needed around here, we may be indicating how little we understand the situation. This can detract from our ability to get things done.
- We can seek understanding of the history and the people who contributed to it. We can ask them to tell about it; people are usually willing to. It is on this historical foundation that the organization will build its future.

- Monday-morning quarterbacking is even more tempting in corporations than it is in football. We can avoid assigning blame and instead can attempt to understand, so that we can help the corporation move into the future.
- Part of respecting history is spending time in it. We can make a special effort to find out what has gone on in the past. Reading reports and files tells us how the organization has operated, added to face-to-face contact with the people who made the organization's history. When we learn the culture and the language, we also learn what has made an organization what it is today.

5

*The Work
Consultants Do
and How They Do It*

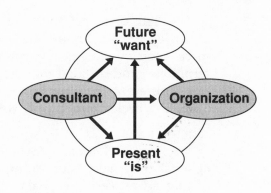

Here Is What We Do . . .

*7*magine for the next few pages that we are partners in consulting. The two of us need a way to communicate with each other about the work we do together, and we need a simple device that will explain our work to our clients—a device that will be useful regardless of the type of project we are working on. I have come up with a four-part model that will help us and our clients understand what we are doing with them. Work through it with me.

With our client organizations we follow a natural work cycle that moves (if you start at three o'clock on the circle) from assessing the situation, to considering the alternatives, to deciding, to action, back to assessment again, and so on, in a continuous learning cycle. (*I think I learned this from someone else so many years ago that I now think I created it. If you know who deserves credit, please tell me. It is further elaborated on in my earlier book,* The Quest for Staff Leadership.)

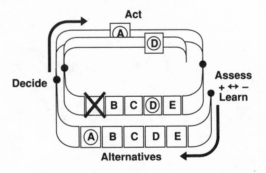

Before we get there, the organizations have taken action and they are uncomfortable with the consequences. They have made their own assessment of the situation, considered their alternatives, and decided that they may be receptive to doing something different that involves us. So they call and we show up. Then the cycle starts again, this time with our influence.

Assess. We help the managers take a deeper look at what they have been doing (action A) and assess the impact of that action on their goals—what they want. Our deeper look involves reaching into areas that the managers who called us were not considering when they analyzed the situation. We seek to understand their present action A more completely; we trace out the consequences (positive to negative) of this action in the organization. We pull all of this information together in a report: "Here is what you have been doing, and here are the consequences of what you have been doing." Negative consequences suggest that alternative actions might be considered. Positive consequences reinforce continuing with action A.

Alternatives. When our clients are unhappy with the consequences of their present actions, we help them develop and consider alternatives. What could be done besides action A? We try to involve people from the organization in developing alternatives, as well as thinking about it a bit on our own. Clients are great contributors to alternatives once they understand their present action and its consequences differently. The largest block to alternatives is being locked in a narrow definition of what is happening now. I remember that old problem analysis proverb, "A problem well defined is halfway to solution."

Decide. Based on the alternative that is generated, we help clients develop an array of possible actions. At this point they do not decide, but are readying themselves to decide. We help them *not* to choose an action too quickly. The "Alternatives" and "Decide" steps in this process are separated to emphasize this. The "Alternatives" step is an opening-up, creative step; the "Decide" step is a closing-down, more evaluative step. The process separates these two steps, recognizing that people's minds work in different ways and that they generally work better if these opening-up and closing-down steps are separate.

The "Decide" step is related to the "Assess" step in that it also uses the larger goals of the organization as criteria. In the "Assess" step, we measure the consequences of action A against goals; in "Decide," we help the client measure the anticipated consequences of alternatives B, C, D, and E against goals. For now, let us say that our client decides on alternative C.

Act. At the top of the cycle, the client implements alternative C; this automatically begins the next cycle, because any action taken will be assessed against goals and intended consequences. And so it goes . . .

What are the advantages of using this model with clients?

- We can explain it quickly.
- They can understand it readily.
- We can tailor it to their situation when discussing actions, assessment, alternatives, and decisions.
- The model is dynamic, always suggesting what may be needed next.
- We can use the model to remind everyone involved where we are in the project.
- The model includes learning from past experience and suggests that we build on that experience. It recognizes that learning never quits.
- We can help them learn to use the model on their own. They do not need us in order to use the model as a guide. We can transfer this small, useful tool to them.

And now that we have worked through the model together, you can use it on your projects with your clients. You don't need me as a partner any longer.

. . . And Here's How I Say It

*L*et's take a look at my typical entry to work with a new client. After hearing the presenting problems from the client, I say, "So it sounds like these are some of the key people involved. What if I go out and talk with them about what's going on?" Simple. Straightforward. Makes sense. Then I go out and talk with people—which often leads me to talk with other people. I take lots of notes. I build reports on what I've heard. This is all part of the assessment of the situation.

I return to the client and say, "When I went out and talked with people, here's what they told me. I've sorted this out according to areas they talked about most and I've listed some of the things they had to say. Let's talk about what it might mean." I give them the report and help them understand it and consider its consequences (to link back to the four-box model). We interpret what it means. Nothing complicated; makes sense. The client sees this step as a natural progression.

This report review is followed by, "Based on what we now know, and what you have been discussing, what are some alternative next steps? It sounds like a logical next step would be to . . ." The opening phrase, "what we now know," is key. My work almost always involves gathering information that results in new knowledge for the client. I can now suggest "logical next steps," building on that new knowledge. The client probably decides to take action because the process has made so much sense to this point.

I recommend to clients what makes sense. It is usually a little different and risky, but it makes sense. I seldom get a reaction where clients say, "What? You must be *crazy!!!*" I try to make sure that what I am proposing makes sense to the client, not just to me.

The clients participate with me in the process. The logical nature of the process allows them to participate fully. It makes sense to them each step of the way.

While helping organizations assess consequences, develop alternatives, decide what to do, and take action, I find myself expressing some common messages over and over again. My words may vary from one company culture to another, but my messages are strikingly similar:

"You people work hard!"
"You are doing important work."
"I respect what you are doing."
"I would like to help."
"You can trust me."
"Let's figure out what is happening now."
"Let's figure out what you want to have happening in the future."
"You are smart people."
"Let's figure out what to do about the difference between what
   you've got and what you want."
"You already know most of what you need to know to make
   the changes you want to make."
"You are doing a good job."
"I like working around here!"

So I run around organizations saying things like that. Undoubtedly I have more basic messages, but these are the messages

I find myself repeating in various ways. No, they do not all hold true for all clients all of the time. When they are true, I try to remember to say them. These statements seem to appeal to people.

The "homeliness" of this approach is also a shortcoming. I have been told by clients that initially they wondered, "If this guy is this down-to-earth, this easy to understand, can he really be bringing us anything new?" Clients often expect more of an expert aura than I project. This has lost me some work. My approach lacks the authority of a well-researched model. There is no special vocabulary to learn; there are no multicolored brochures. There is just me, my experience, and my readiness to put myself to work in their organization.

6

Guiding Yourself in the Present

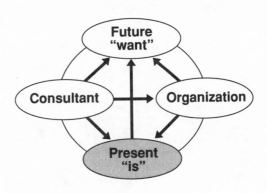

*T*his is about helping organizations open to change, moving from the Present: "is" to the Future: "want." It comes in two chapters. "Guiding Yourself in the Present" is the more immediate of the two, providing thoughts that can rest in the front of your mind while you are working on a change project today. "Guiding Yourself Toward the Future" is more idealistic, feeding your thoughts about the meaning of your work. These thoughts may wander around the back of your mind, occasionally being called forth as you ponder the significance of what you have been doing.

While running around the cycles of the Assess-Alternatives-Decide-Act model with clients, I have collected core thoughts on how to bring about change. (*Earlier short lists from Stan Herman, Herb Shepard, and Marvin Weisbord inspired this section.*) I put them in a list: the "consulting wisdom" I try to follow while I work. I can recall most of them from memory; they keep me on track—when I follow their guidance. Taken in combination, they define the profile of the kind of consultant I want to be today for my clients. First, the list; then the elaboration.

Consulting Wisdom
- The work begins here.
- Simple works.
- Get out of the way.
- Change hurts.
- Risk as you expect others to risk.
- Create context.
- Seed hope.
- Persevere.
- Find the client in yourself.
- You are your best intervention.

The Work Begins Here

*N*o matter where you are in the consulting process, getting to someplace else starts right here! There is simply no place else to start. As obvious as that may sound to some of you, it certainly is not always that obvious to me. Some examples of my avoiding what needs to be done now: when I have great ideas about what could happen next in a company, but the client is scared to take action; or when I hope for a client company that is more enlightened than the one I am working with; or when I gripe about the client organization's culture and lament that it is so autocratic.

These three examples all avoid the point: The work begins here! Reminding myself of that grounds me. My action orientation is engaged; the resourceful and practical me moves into motion. Now I am ready to do something, not just dream about different futures, clients, or organizations.

Dreaming about alternatives often symbolizes an internal rejection of the real starting point. It is the idealistic me playing in a fantasy world that does not have to face reality. It is a world of perfect clients and perfect organizations, and I am (what else?) the perfect consultant. The one major flaw is that a perfect client in a perfect world would not need perfect consultants! Poof! and back to reality: My starting point is with this client organization with its warts and opportunities, problems and possibilities. Accepting that reality allows me to embrace the work rather than avoid it.

Simple Works

*I*magine that you are a change agent, trying to live up to your label, consulting to the management of an organization of three thousand people with six levels of hierarchy in five major divisions across four states making and selling the same products they have made for the last fifteen years. How do you talk with, work with, this company? Messages full of subtlety delivered to this organization are doomed. Memos containing twenty-three action points will be lost. Well-intentioned presidential prose will evaporate. Try simple. Simple works.

Whether it is a company of three thousand or a board meeting of twenty or a task team of six, when you are working on change, simple works. I am saying this to all of us who love twelve-box models, and subtlety, and research, and eloquence. As useful as that might be at a professional meeting or a cocktail party, it needs to be shelved in favor of what works to bring about change. And what works? Simple, as in 1-2-3.

- Do clients the service of helping them distill their communications down to the most essential points.
- Search out the profoundly simple approach.
- Seek ways of presenting your message in an uncluttered fashion.
- Distill required actions down to their most fundamental elements.
- Find the core of what you want and communicate that.
- Remove the tail fins, hubcaps, fender skirts, and sun visor; strip it down to its essentials.
- Allow the nobility of the core design to show through.
- Whether it is a meeting, a recommendation, or a reorganization, unclutter your approach to the work.

Bringing about change in a company of the size, depth, width, geography, and history we have described requires exceptional clarity. How many changes can three thousand people absorb, together, at the same time? When there are six levels of hierarchy, how many actions can they own and take together? When the organization is spread across five divisions and four states, only a few core change messages can be carried effectively.

An organization that normally is adept at communicating routine business goes "tilt" when faced with communication of "abnormal" change information. The changes we are supporting need to be participated in, understood, owned, and acted upon by the people in the organization. All of this involvement also argues for simplicity and lack of complication. No, not a meat-axe approach, not a crude or insensitive method, but an appropriate and profound simplification.

Start with the assumption that change is complex and anything we can do to simplify it appropriately is helpful. We hope to create support for our efforts, not to provide our detractors with ammunition. Complexity is ammunition. Try these stimulators of simplicity. Ask yourself:

- What one thing do they want to do together? If you don't know, find out. If they don't know, help them realize it.

- What would you have them do right now? If you don't know, figure it out. If they don't know, tell them.
- What unites them? Ask yourself. Ask them.

These questions cut through complexity; they serve to unify, to bind groups of people. They overlay diverse groups and individuals with common thoughts and actions.

I want to simplify, not "complexify," what is happening in the client organization. I'm usually called because of the complexity the client faces. For me to come in and make it even more complex is not the best service. Somehow, by understanding and action, I want to make the situation more manageable for the client.

Sometimes I worry that I am simplifying not because the situation calls for it, but because I am not smart enough to handle the confusion. That is a real possibility. On the other hand, I know that what is difficult for me to understand is probably also difficult for many other people caught up in a difficult situation. Invariably when I check I find that this is true; my intuition is supported by experience. This encourages me to continue my search for simple expression and simple action.

From another perspective, the world is very complex, even chaotic. I help myself through this confusion by drawing simple mental maps that keep me focused and on track. I try to do the same thing for my clients.

Get Out of the Way

*G*etting out of the way means letting clients run their own organizations. It means continuing to be a consultant, not a manager. It means celebrating their accomplishments. It means keeping your mouth shut while they learn. It means helping them learn rather than doing their work. It requires patience, humility, and self-confidence.

I often get in the way. In the process of helping people in the organization do their work better, my need for recognition can become a barrier to my effectiveness and their progress. My demonstrations of skill, wisdom, creativity, cleverness, and humor divert us from the task at hand. In retrospect I can see many situations where I was trying to get attention rather than trying to help. I was worried as hell that they would not see that I was important to what they were doing. Or I was scared they would find out that they didn't need me. My grand anxiety is that I am putting myself in service to other people and nobody wants my help! So, then, where does that leave me? I'd rather not think about it.

There is truth in that old proverb, "You can get anything done, if you don't worry about who gets the credit." Pursuing personal credit is especially detrimental to consultants. We are already in the favored, special position of having been called in to help the organization. People are looking to us for guidance. They give us unusual powers in their organizations. An exaggerated need for recognition and credit can compound the problem of clients' dependence on us. We can end up in decision-making roles and responsibilities that really belong to the clients—all because our need for credit pushed us into doing their job.

The answer (for me) has been to increase my personal satisfaction with contributing to others' accomplishment. When I measure myself against my own standards, I can reward myself for what I have done. This is a much more reliable source of recognition than those outside of me. I do get a great kick from watching and helping people learn to deal with their work in more effective ways. I do feel great satisfaction when people I have worked with see their work from a life, not just a company, perspective. I love to hear about clients helping others in ways that I helped them. The subtle side of consulting has more appeal to me now—enabling others to develop their vision, their mission, their strategy; knowing that a group is more focused and committed than it has ever been; seeing a manager discover the impact of her behavior on the people around her. These are all indicators that I have made a difference.

I recognize the bind I place myself in when on the one hand I say, "Get out of the way!" and on the other I say, "Facilitation is not enough: Lead!" I think the resolution of this apparent contradiction is in your and my motives. Consider your motive for what you are doing with the client: Is it centered on accomplishment for the organization or attention for yourself? Put another way, is your motive directed outward or inward? Honestly answering that question can provide the resolution you and I need.

Change Hurts

7 have tried to think of some other way to say it. Change is uncomfortable, difficult, and irritating. None of those words captures the depth of the change experience. Hurt is often used in association with harm and damage and pain, all negative words. Though change can be harmful and damaging to the organization and the people in it, that is not the kind of change or hurt I am referring to. I believe that positive, healthy change usually hurts. It hurts the way your muscles hurt when you ask them to do something they are not used to doing; it hurts the way it does when your child has less time for you or when you must deal with aging parents.

Change does not always hurt, but if it comes quickly and is important, it does. Gradual change over years rather than weeks will hurt less noticeably. The changes consultants help with usually happen in a short time and therefore hurt. Organizations and individuals often choose to change. That does not eliminate the hurt; choice just makes it more acceptable.

Certainly there are changes that are joyous for some parts of the organization, but there is probably someplace else in the company that suffers from a change in its old ways of doing things. Recognizing that people may see the change you represent as hurtful helps you deal empathetically with them. Acting as if all will be sweetness and light after a change is to neglect the feelings of the people affected by it. Singing an entirely positive refrain to a room full of gloomy people is ignoring an important reality.

So we need to allow for the hurt that comes with change and build care into our change processes. We who thrive on change—at least on helping *others* change—might forget what it is like to be on the receiving end of our fine work.

Risk as You Expect Others to Risk

7 hink of a client you have dealt with recently. Think of someone with a major opportunity to move forward, an opportunity that requires significant risk. The potential gains are large, but so is the risk when it is looked at from the client's perspective. Imagine how the client sees this risky opportunity. Imagine how much risk that client faces. Now, are you willing to risk *as much* to help that client? Will you put yourself on the line to the same extent as the client does?

An example: Recently three of us, two executives from a telecommunications company and myself, designed a strategic planning session for the top four management levels of the company, about 200 managers. In one four-hour session, we had arranged for teams of managers to offer their ideas about strategic directions and operational plans to vice-presidents of the company; further, all of their ideas would be collected and used as input to future planning. To increase the energy and fun, our design had all of this happening in a kind of board game/game show format with lots of color and balloons and noise. Each team of managers had noisemakers (horns, whistles, etc.) to show appreciation with, or declare their existence, or whatever.

Can you visualize what we designed? Picture a kind of planned planning pandemonium! We were excited about our ideas and nervous about the wilder aspects of the design. We saw it as a risk and we all had something on the line. The company had never sponsored a meeting like this; I had never led one quite like this before. I was willing to lead it if the company was willing to sponsor it. My risk matched theirs.

I felt fortunate to have a client that was willing to take risks with me. Often clients hire me to do something that I have successfully done before—in fact, they do not want me to risk. I am their insurance as they risk doing something that is new for them. Clients who encourage me to do something new provide learning for me.

One way in which I judge how much I am risking is by the success of the projects I work on. A strong pattern of success, say 95 percent, can suggest that I have room to take much more risk than I am taking. Success might seem a silly thing to be concerned about, but in relation to risk, growth, and creativity, overwhelming success may be a negative indicator. If your work "always works" for you, then take a look at how much you are risking and how much you are learning.

Another risky point: We often hang on to our own perspective on risk and lose the client's perspective. It's analogous to watching someone build up the nerve to leap a five-foot chasm. If we have made the leap frequently and if we have guided many others in safe leaps, five feet is not much of a risk for us. But *this* person is on the edge right now, facing a new situation loaded with risk for him. See it from his perspective. What would be a similar test for us? How about an eight-foot gap? No? Then let's say it's a ten-foot chasm. Knowing that our own risk level is at ten feet, what kind of support would we like in order to attempt such a leap? That is the level of support we should bring to the person attempting five feet.

A last example: A person who is not used to confronting her boss may find it to be an extremely difficult process. I am used to that; you are used to that. We have been confronting bosses for years. What is really hard for us may be confronting ourselves. We should bring to the person confronting her boss the kind of support we would like to have as we confront ourselves. Providing support to someone who is risking is a critical part of our work. I think we too often are oblivious to the risks being taken, effectively discouraging the risk taker. We act as if the risk being taken is not a risk, but normal. This encourages the risker to act "normal" and not to acknowledge what she is going through, depriving herself of support.

Create Context

7 build new contexts for people. I help them be themselves, but in different surroundings. This is one of the main things I do for my clients. What surrounds them is different from what it was a moment ago, allowing them to come up with new perspectives, insights, and decisions. They use the same knowledge, skills, and abilities they use each day, but in a different context. In effect, they become consultants to themselves.

How does context get changed? Here are three examples:

1. In reading this book, you are stepping into a different context. You have your own context for consulting; you have chosen to step into mine. As you read, you are seeing what you already know in relation to what I know.
2. Six sales managers are redefining their jobs. I ask each of them to write down the most important contributions a sales manager makes or could make to the organization. I have them write each of these potential contributions on a separate sheet of paper boldly, with a felt marker. Then I ask them to lay

these pages on the floor around them for all to see. Last of all, I have them sort and discuss their work, looking for patterns and discussing the importance of the contributions. By doing this, I have helped them create a new context to think and work within—they are even surrounded by this new context.

3. A group of supervisors is troubled about the motivation of their employees. They want to learn how to motivate them. I ask the supervisors to pair up, to go out and meet with groups of employees (not their own), and to ask those groups to tell the supervisors what motivates them. The pairs do this and come back with far more information than they ever expected was available to them, which they put up in writing for all the supervisors to see. No new skills, just a new context in which people can work with each other in a different way than they usually do.

There is a pattern in these examples: "We have been acting within one framework. Let's see what happens when we act within another!" That is shifting context. How do we get there?

Generally, I try to imagine a new context in which it would be useful for these people to work. What would it be useful for them to be surrounded by? I engage them in considering the possibilities and help them create that new setting. Then I ask them to step into this new setting to do their work. In the three examples given here, readers stepped into books, sales managers surrounded themselves with their own ideas, and supervisors surrounded themselves with employees' ideas. These surroundings caused people to work differently than they had in the past.

The possibilities for shifting context are endless, but here are a few more examples:

- Hold longer meetings with a problem-solving agenda.
- Adjust the planning process so that operational plans are assessed quarterly against the mission.
- Redesign an individual job to include more decisions.
- Adjust the work flow within the group.
- Gather and discuss data on group morale.
- Rearrange the office to affect communication.
- Provide daily feedback on production.

Each of these possibilities has to do with adjusting the space, system, or structure within which work is done. All are context rather than the basic content of the work. The output is the same; the way it is produced changes.

Seed Hope

*O*ne of the primary commodities I bring to clients is hope. Clients need to believe, "We can do something about this!" As important as action plans are, they are nothing without the creation of hope; without it, all the planned actions will be likely to remain just plans.

Hope comes when new perspectives generate new alternatives. Clients often call when they have already tried everything they can think of. It is common for them to feel stuck, if not hopelessly stuck. Suggestions of actions within their old perspective usually result in responses such as, "We've already tried that." "That won't work because . . ." "They won't let us do that." "We can't do that in this company." At this point, I usually begin to feel that it is pretty hopeless, too. I get stuck along with them—maybe it really is not possible to do anything about the problem.

Just before I despair, my hopeful bias saves me! I begin to look at the organization through other eyes. I help people get their eyes off their present problems and focused on the way they would like things to be. I help them create visions of their desired future. I ask them to create on paper the organization they want to work for. And as we all focus on the possible future, hope is created. Hope becomes the knowledge that this company can be changed, that we can do something about the problems, that it is worth our effort, that what we want can be achieved here. And furthermore, we are willing to do something about it! This is the point where the hopes that have become a common vision move into action and realization.

Seeding an organization with hope—that is another way of looking at it. The process involves:

Helping people understand the difference between what they
   have and what they want
Helping them see that they can do something to bring about
   change
Aiding them in the creation of visions of the organization they
   want to work in
Bringing them some ways of gaining new perspectives and new
   alternatives
Facilitating their expression of what they want to accomplish
   together
Building actions that show their progress out of their problems

These are examples of seeding hope. As people take responsibility, as they act together, and as they see old problems
in new ways, they grow hopeful. And the hope they grow seeds
new efforts, new actions, and new hope.
   Yes, there is such a thing as a hopeless situation that deserves to be abandoned. There are situations where the chances
of improvement are so small that they do not deserve to be invested in. Seeding hope here is irresponsible. You have to decide
whether to invest yourself and whether to encourage others to
invest.
   Before overloading you with the importance of a positive
attitude, it is time for some griping, whining, complaining, and
moaning. Ready? I mean, *I have had it* with all this hope-filled
rubbish! Let's talk *reality* for a few lines! You should see some
of the people I have to work with! And the antiquated structures
they call organizations! And the ways they communicate! The
myth of delegation! The egos of some of their executives! I mean,
things are really screwed up!! Let's go out for a beer and I will
really tell you about it! I'm feeling better already.
   Do not put aside all of those things that are wrong, unjust,
broken, unfair, mistaken, crazy, out of whack, or otherwise
messed up. Continue to gripe about the problems you have with
the traditional organizational structure. Keep railing about the stupidity of the decision-making system. Continue complaining
about the client's style. This is valid and it feels good to bitch
about it. It doesn't accomplish much but it does feel good, especially over a beer.
   And in addition (here comes the positive approach):

- Give yourself credit for how much you accomplished this week.
- Brag (softly) about the project team you helped that turned out such great results so fast.
- Commend the management team for the way it handled that difficult problem yesterday.
- Sing the praises of the CEO for the strategic leadership provided.
- Talk about the parts of this work that you *love* to do.
- Look to the future; talk about what "can be" and not just "what is."
- Accentuate the positive in your discussions within client organizations.
- When interviewing people, ask them what is working well. Ask them what they like about their jobs. Ask them what their boss does especially well. Ask them what their company does that makes them proud. And continue to ask them about what is less effective, what is wrong, and what needs improvement.
- Help your clients build appreciation into organizational systems, especially systems that recognize individual, team, or work-unit performance. Argue to have accomplishments extolled, not taken for granted.
- Elaborate on how well an individual performs.
- Learn from all the good work that goes into top performance by examining it.
- Praise accomplishment in person, at banquets, at meetings, in newsletters, and on videotape.

All of this deserves to be heard, just as the problems facing our clients deserve to be heard. None of this is very hard to do and it is so much more satisfying than a constant preoccupation with what is wrong. Some of us deal with the positive as if it were in contradiction to the negative—a kind of "yeah, but" perspective. The positive and the negative are both true. They stand beside each other, each giving their own evidence about performance. One does not add to or subtract from the other; they are both real, and they each deserve recognition.

Persevere

I am in this work for the long haul. And I am in this client system for the long haul. Recently a plant manager told his staff, "Deal with Geoff as though he were going to be here for years. See him as a resource available to you whenever you need him. He is not here to work on a single project, but on long-term change." That timeline has a profound effect on our work. It reduces my impatience and requires my perseverance. My actions in that plant are positively different because of the long-term commitment of my client and myself.

Effective organizational change is not accomplished through a series of one-night consulting stands. Effective consultation requires us to build a relationship for the long term, as in a marriage. The client and the consultant invest in more than just the present event; they see this event as part of what has happened and what will happen. Hanging in there for the long term produces a deep knowledge of how the organization moves and breathes. It results in interventions that are attuned to how the organization actually lives, rather than how we imagine it works. This requires that we work through the less glorious, less momentous times. It is patience-testing, commitment-testing work that can produce growth.

Choosing to pursue this long-term relationship assures me of some hard times as I help clients struggle with their issues. For my "troubles," I will learn about the organization in depth; I will learn its culture, rituals, norms, systems, and people. I will be called upon to help with opportunities and problems I have not faced before. I will not always be helpful; sometimes my work will get in the way. I will risk and learn in the process. All of this is what comes with a long-term commitment to a client. It is through persevering with clients over years that I have made my most significant contributions and learned the most.

Find the Client in Yourself

*F*rom one perspective, all the work I do, I do within myself. All that work with clients "out there" is really done "in here," because "in here" is the only place where I can bring together whatever is going on "out there." (Nod your head if you are still with me.) If that is true, I can be effective with clients only to the extent that I can make them part of me. Somehow, I must become them or find them in a part of myself. So, because it all happens "in here," all my work with clients is work with parts of me. (If you are not still with me, please read this first paragraph again, because it is a lead-in to an important point.)

To a great extent my success in fully understanding clients depends on having had experiences like the ones they are having, especially at the feeling level. When I can show clients that I understand them at an intellectual, emotional, physical, and spiritual level, I have found them "in here." When I can demonstrate their thoughts or feelings to them, when I can accurately interpret how they might handle a situation, then I know I am ready to help. I "become" the client; I "am" the problem, the dilemma, the opportunity, the contradiction—whatever it is that the client brought to me.

So when I am working with a client on an issue, I search for the client within myself. I try to find those parts of me that are like the client. I test the client to see if I am understanding and I test myself to find the client in me. When I find that part of me which is like the client, I notice my reactions to it. Do I like what I have found? It is not always comfortable; sometimes I am repulsed by what I find.

Here is a recurrent example; it has come up in some form at least twenty times. I am working with a group of people who are very reactive to the larger organization they are part of, and who are angry about being "put in this position." According to them, management only tells them when they do things wrong and never tells them what they are supposed to do. Furthermore, they cannot change things because no one listens to them. In addition, they do not get the respect in the organization they deserve. They probably ought to report to a higher level, too. This is all said with some petulant anger, even a whining tone. If you have consulted to more than ten groups, I am sure you have run into this one.

As they talk I search for similar experiences in myself—and I do not have to search very hard. Their complaints sound very much like some I voiced years back when I was an employee. I do not have to imagine much to identify with this client group. I also notice the anger I have at management and at an organization that doesn't respect or use me as I'd like to be used. I feel abused, unappreciated, unheard, not respected, and angry! I tell the group this and they encourage me. Now we are all in the same pickle! My advantage is that I chose to be here with them temporarily and I have experience with coming in and getting out. I search within my angry, abused self and find something that initially I didn't notice: I am angry at others, but I am also angry at myself for putting up with all this garbage! I begin to recognize that I have chosen to accept the limits I imagined others were imposing on me, and I have not tested those limits. In a word, I have chosen to be a victim! Recognizing my responsibility in this is a first step to getting out of this mess I am in. And helping the client group do the same is a first step for them.

So by finding the client "in here," I can find alternative paths that help that client "out there." There are important side benefits to this approach:

- The clients know that I understand very well what is going on with them.
- They can see my acceptance of them and their situation. They hear me talking about having related experiences and they hear me laughing at myself, sometimes even at my own stupidity or my mistakes or my weakness.
- The combination of my understanding and acceptance of them helps them to be open to considering alternative actions or changes they might make to get out of the fix they are in.

You Are Your Best Intervention

*T*he techniques I use, the designs I create, and the recommendations I put forth are all potentially useful. The new ways of thinking, the alternative perspectives, the new context—these are all valuable. But they often pale by comparison to the fact of my presence, to being there. Check this against your own experience. (*The seed of this wisdom was planted in me* *by Marvin Weisbord years ago. It took a while for it to grow and flower; now it is in full bloom.*)

When I am in the room, a client group holds a better meeting than when I am not—even if I don't do anything. Clients behave differently because I am there, not just because of what I do. This observation is reinforced when others say, "That was really a good meeting today; thanks for your help." Or "That session would have gone a lot differently if you hadn't been there." Or "Thanks to you, we are really making progress!" The striking thing about each of these comments is that they were said following meetings in which I did very little.

It is as if we consultants become minor totems. We stand for what the organization strives for; therefore, the people invested in this striving behave differently around us. Or perhaps it is like being on one's best behavior when company comes or behaving well in the presence of a person "of the cloth."

A related story: Last week a client told me about a series of decisions she had managed particularly well and was very proud of. She attributed much of her success to her work with me because during the process she asked herself, "What would Geoff suggest that I do?" She described all that I would have suggested and how she followed these "suggestions" successfully. I listened, impressed with the innovative steps she had taken, and congratulated her on her accomplishment. I also told her that what she had done was much more effective and creative than what I probably would have recommended. This amazed her; she thought she was doing just what I would have recommended.

I understand what she did because I have used other consultants in the same way. I often think, "What would Mike do in this situation?" and then imagine the actions that Mike Di-Lorenzo, a friend and associate, would take. Bringing his perspective into my own broadens my thinking and options. His phantom presence is a guide I can choose to follow.

You can see the relationship between this imagined presence and the real presence of a consultant. In both examples the consultant was present (even if it was only in the client's mind) and silent. The client created a silent interaction with the consultant that affected the client's actions. The consultants, by not doing anything, did a lot.

7

Guiding Yourself Toward the Future

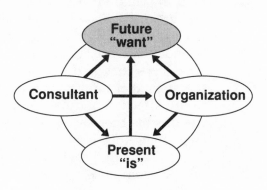

*W*hat you are about to read floats a few feet above and ahead of the day-to-day concerns of consulting. It links the practical with the ideal, ensuring that today's actions are moves toward the larger meanings of tomorrow. It is the possible future calling out to us and our clients as we work, saying, "Remember what you want out of life!" It is most relevant to our work; it informs what we do and brings meaning and value to our work life.

As consultants, we have the opportunity to help people work toward the futures they want. We have the challenge of helping them release themselves from their addiction to the present, an addiction that prevents them from getting what they say they want. And of course, we struggle with the same compelling issue even as we try to assist our clients. We'll begin with a children's story.

Imagine, along with me, that you have children just entering high school. Wonderful children with potential—not perfect children, but smart, able, healthy, warm individuals. You have a parent's hopes and dreams for them. When they are thirty, what would you like to be saying about them? Mentally note your answers before reading further.

Here are a few of my answers: I hope they are happy, are in good health, have friends, are educated and wise, love their family, are doing work that they find fulfilling, have found a solid life partner, are good citizens, are independent, have options in their lives—and are not living with their parents!

Because that list is important to me, I will work toward it. In fact, most of my actions with my children are aimed at making this list a reality for each of them. I will reach, and will help my children reach, for these dreams. Although I know that the dreams I have for my children cannot be accomplished or reached in the sense that I can go out and acquire happiness, or independence, or health, or options for them, there are tangible steps they and I can take toward those dreams. I can measure steps that I am taking, or they are taking, that seem to move in the direction of those important dreams, but I cannot measure the dreams themselves. I can only value them and take the concrete steps that I think lead to them.

Paying for their college education supports the life options and wisdom and happiness I want them to have. A college education is measurable, although it is not what is most important. While they are in high school, I can measure whether my kids are going to school each day, have friends, are participating in sports, and get decent grades. Today, right now, we want them to turn off the TV and take out the trash. We help them reach for the lofty long-term visions by encouraging them in the present. We don't say, "I want you to be happy, helpful, and industrious so I am asking you to take out the trash." But that is what we mean. We see the connection between our visions and what is happening today in the kitchen. The lofty visions are not measurable; today's actions are. But as we focus on today's actions, we risk losing our own (and our children's) perspective on why these actions are important.

My next six points are closely connected to this children's story. We will be talking about organizations' futures and clients' dreams instead of children's futures and our dreams. We will explore how we can help clients realize the futures they want; we will wrestle with the difficulties of planning for a work world that does not yet exist.

Values and Visions and Importance

*W*e can help ourselves and our clients move from the Present: "is" to the Future: "want" by focusing on values and visions. When we and they are clear about what we believe in, when we can envision the future we want to create, we have made a significant step toward realizing that future. Having vision and values clarifies the future work world we are trying to create and the beliefs we will honor as we create that work world. No, it does not give us knowledge, skill, or experience, but with this greater guidance in place we will be better prepared.

Let's discuss values and vision long enough to have a common sense of what they are and how they are important. Our vision is the world we are trying to create and our values are the beliefs we honor as we reach out for that world. I will talk about them together because they are inseparable in our work.

Importance has to do with sorting out what is most compelling, most necessary, to the world we are creating; it has to do with decisions about planning, and action, and progress.

First values, then vision, then importance . . .

On the Value of "Why?"

*A*t the risk of sounding like a three-year-old, ask the question *why?* of anything you do. And note the answer. Then ask *why?* again. And note the answer. And again. And again. It does not take long before you are moved from the realm of knowledge into the realm of beliefs. You soon reach the point where you have no further explanation; you just believe it. For example:

"I am a consultant."
"Why?"
"I want to have a positive impact on the organizations people work within."
"Why?"
"I want people to have the opportunity to use their human talents in their work."
"Why?"
"Because life is short and work is a significant part of life and it is a potentially rich place for human expression."
"Why?"
"I believe that we are each here to give expression to our potential, to grow into our fuller selves."
"Why?"
"I have no more reasons; I just believe that."

This short exchange exposes one underlying belief that I bring to my work. It tells the listener that I want to see people's talents expressed through their work; you can expect that perspective to be reflected in how I approach my consulting work.

Values come from the heart; people live by them. These are not rules of behavior; rules come from the mind. Values are beliefs, not rules. I encourage clients to express their underlying beliefs and values as they explore what they want from the future. These beliefs will guide them as they move into the future and will shape the future they envision. The image that just came to mind is of the early Pilgrim settlers of this country who were held together by common, deeply held beliefs. These beliefs would have been important to their future regardless of where they settled. In a less dramatic way, clients' values shape their behavior and influence the vision they create.

The reasons behind our actions, and organizations' actions, need more discussion than they ordinarily get today. I think that the rash of ethical problems we have seen around Wall Street and Capitol Hill are there because the *why* questions are not asked enough. Actions lose their connection with principles and underlying beliefs. Our fascination with the *how* obliterates discussions of the *why*. We can lead our clients to a larger perspective by helping them understand their reasons.

Envision, If You Will . . .

*W*hen teaching people to ski (or play tennis, or golf) some instructors use visualization in building skills. They ask you to picture yourself skiing well and to learn from those internal pictures. They might ask you to close your eyes, picture yourself skiing, feel the skis under your feet, hear the skis move through the snow, feel the wind in your face, and see your body over your skis. They then ask you to be the skier you have envisioned.

In a similar fashion, you can make a mental movie of the way you want to live and work and then move out into the world to create the movie that is in your mind. Make decisions that move you toward a reality like the one you have in mind. Take actions that are like those you have in mind. Express yourself in ways that are consistent with what you have in mind. The mental movie, watched regularly, reminds you of what is important to you.

As a consultant, you can help others express and create the futures they want. You can use your talents to help others understand what they want to build together. You can encourage them to give time to their corporate dreams. And you can make it more legitimate to talk about visions and values. Visioning offers a way to help you do this.

At the time when I am writing this book, it seems as if all sorts of people are trying to find out what visioning can do for them. They are writing visions, publishing them, touting them, becoming enthusiastic over them. It seems that visioning is what you are supposed to be doing right now. The faddish aspects of it bother me. I am worried that the power of creating a vision will be lost in the promotion.

Visions of the future have been important in the creation of hope, as discussed earlier in this chapter. Visions build motivation in those who see a common future. And, apart from what is happening in the life of large organizations, vision has always been a source of strength for individuals, as was described in the example of parents' hopes for their children.

Visionary people make decisions in the present based on the world they want to create. They bring it to reality by creating it, bit by bit, each day. They are very practical people; they pay close attention to what is happening around them in order to affect what is happening. They use their vision of what they want in the future, not just the pictures of the past, to determine their actions. Visions legitimize thoughts, feelings, and action that just don't find a place under a more rational, number-centered management system.

If It Is Important, You Cannot Measure It

*T*he prevailing "wisdom" of corporate life says that if you cannot measure it, it is not important. I disagree. I believe that if it is important, you cannot measure it. The really important things in life cannot be measured, made tangible, quantified, packaged, boxed, or tied down. In fact, the most important things in life are not "things" at all. What we want out of life is not for sale, for lease, or for rent. How could you quantify these moments?

A young man and young woman have been going together for three years and were engaged to be married six months ago. Today they are marrying in a big church ceremony with their families and friends in attendance. They have been looking forward to this moment for a long time. They feel a deep love for each other as they commit to living the rest of their lives together. Neither of them can think of anything more important that has ever happened to them.

A management team has successfully created a common vision of what they want this organization to become. They also have created a common understanding of what their mutual role is in bringing this vision to reality. They are all emotionally inspired by what they have done together, their spirits are higher than they have ever been, and they are excited about the future they are going to create. This is the most important team experience in their careers.

A work group of five employees steps back from their daily routine to look at their work and consider alternative ways of accomplishing it. After many meetings and long discussion, they decide to change the work process and their individual jobs. As one result, they agree that they can do the work with three people rather than five. They recommend this change to management, noting which people want to leave the group and where they would like to work in the organization. The group feels unified and very professional as a result of their work together; they are thrilled with their accomplishment. They see this as the most innovative work they have done in years. They are excited as they begin working within their new design.

We could ask the people in these three experiences to complete questionnaires, to submit to interviews, to report to us on what they have done together and how they felt about what they have done. The data could be useful to us as indicators of what happened, but they would not *be* what happened. The only way to know fully what happened would be to experience it.

Counter to management by objectives, bottom-line thinking, and the widget watchers of the western world, the essence of our most meaningful experiences is not quantifiable, measurable, or tangible. Yes, we can collect quantifiable data about the experience, but that is different from the experience itself. We cannot put calipers on a dream, on happiness, on excitement, on motivation. The essence is being in the experience, not standing outside measuring it. As useful as measurement might be, it remains outside the world it is assessing. And we forget that. We confuse the measurement with the experience.

Here is what I see us doing, and by "us," I mean consultants and clients. We lose track of why we are measuring what we are measuring; we just do not ask *why* anymore. Instead we concentrate on *how* and *what*. We know what to do and how to do it, and we just do the job, over and over again. With time the *why* question fades from our minds and hearts. We look around us at work and see others busily engaged in doing the same thing, so how wrong could we be? We measure ourselves against them, or what we did last year, or what we plan to do this year, but not against the question *why*. We measure what is easier to measure, rather than what is important. Some of us begin to think that our measures are important; we lose sight of what they were designed to support.

- If you find yourself bound up in the measurable or tied up with numbers, know that they may be indicators pointing to what is important. We have created all these numbers to keep track of it—whatever "it" is.

- If you find yourself working to achieve something measurable for its own sake, without regard for what it is contributing to, know that you have narrowed yourself and blocked other larger perspectives.

- If you find yourself arguing with a client about numbers and saying that they really are not what is most important, know that you are on the right track but using the wrong methods. This is not an argument against numbers; it is an argument for using them rather than being used by them.

- If you find yourself ignoring numbers that your clients are enamored with, know that you are at risk. Keep in mind where these numbers are pointing. If they are pointing to another number, where is that number pointing? Keep searching until you find a level that no one has yet put numbers on or made tangible in some other measurable way. Search until the core reasons have to be explained to you rather than being "self-evident" in the statistics. Then you probably will have reached the dreams, the vision, the values of the organization. That, simply, is what is important. That is what the numbers unsuccessfully try to capture.

All of this is designed to put measurement in a life perspective, a perspective that is easy to lose in the midst of a business world that prizes next quarter's numbers and this year's profits. In the midst of the corporate game, our clients may lose their larger sense of life direction. They are bombarded with measurements of what they have achieved, are achieving, and ought to achieve in relation to important business matters—which may or may not be related to important life matters.

Who are we to shake our heads and cluck about perspectives lost? Retaining a life perspective on our work is a most difficult and profound talent for us to bring to our clients and to ourselves. We have the advantage of not being a permanent part of their corporation's culture, so we can look in from the outside; some perspective must come with that. We also have the disadvantage of not being a permanent part of any corporation's culture, so we may lack the solid support our perspective needs.

Money and Happiness

7 am concerned about the limits that measurement may put on my vision and values. Measurements give us useful, widely agreed-upon indicators of our progress toward what is important to us. The measure is not what is important; the progress is. For example, supposing that you tell me you are happy and successful in your life because you are now making $300,000 a year. I have a few questions:

What do you want out of your life?
What are you doing with your life now that you were not doing before you had all this money?
How is the money essential in getting what you want out of your life?

You will surely come up with some good answers to these questions and I will be able to understand how the options provided by the money have made you happy and successful. The dollar amount alone is a useful, readily understood indicator, but it is not happiness or success.

If you want $300,000 a year, your options are limited to those that make money. If you want happiness and success, you have many options—including raising a happy family, opening a bookstore, becoming a gourmet cook, opening a day care center, and being a successful consultant, as well as all of the other options that include money. Our grander hopes and dreams can be reached by many paths. Whether we want happiness, success, wisdom, love, or realization of our potential, there are many ways of getting there.

The narrower your vision, the fewer are the alternatives to move toward it: "I'd be so happy if I won the lottery." "I'd be happy if I had a new car." "With a college diploma, I would be happy forever." Look at how few paths there are toward a lottery win, a car, or a diploma in comparison with the paths to wisdom, love, or realization of one's potential. In fact, we reach for those larger dreams by creating smaller ones. We choose to narrow our reach to a few of the many options available. The key word here is *choose*. While we make the choice we maintain the connection. We don't lose ourselves in the education or the car; we remind ourselves that these goals serve the larger *whys* of our life meaning.

What we bring to ourselves, we also bring to our clients. We help them to realize and maintain the connection between what is happening today and their life meaning. We help them see how today's work serves their visions. We come in from the outside with a perspective that is outside of and beyond work.

When working with clients on important directions, I encourage them to seek out measurable progress indicators on their most important and lofty dreams, values, visions, and goals. If a goal is highly important, we want to keep track of our movement toward it. The more important it is, the more we want to keep track of it. As we track our success, we must remind ourselves that we are not measuring for the sake of measurement, but because we want indicators of our progress toward something unmeasurable and important.

In Pursuit of the Unmeasurably Important

*H*ow do we help our clients and ourselves pursue what is both important and unmeasurable? If it were measurable, it would be easy: "We sold 6,799 units last quarter, 15 percent more than last year, and we are really motivated and happy in our work. As the leader, I feel terrific about that!" We all understand "6,799" and "quarter" and "15 percent" in the same way. We know what they mean; we share the same understanding of these numbers. But "motivated" and "happy" and "terrific" are a different matter. Though we all value motivation and happiness and "terrificness," what we mean individually by these words can be quite different. And if we are out promoting work motivation and happiness and "terrificness" across the organization, these feelings will be a damned sight harder to communicate than last quarter's sales figures.

I don't need to tell you again and again what last quarter's unit sales were. I can probably tell you once and you will remember in a way that fits precisely with mine, with no argument about it. However, if I say that employees are motivated, our interpretations of what that means are likely to differ greatly. We will agree that motivation is important, but not on what it is. Because motivation is so difficult to tie down, it is even more difficult for us to support it in a large organization. Our structures and systems do much better with quantities than with qualities. We know how to keep track of numbers and are inclined to reinforce that ability rather than to figure out how to support what is unmeasurable and important.

Let's take an example: "We value people." An organization that values the people working for it will need to find a variety of ways of reiterating and demonstrating that value. Saying it once at the annual stockholders' meeting will not do it. Neither will repeating it twice more at retirement dinners, or building it into the introduction to the new management training program. As well intentioned as these separate efforts might be, they do not come close to the daily attention that valuing people requires. The organization can express this value with structures, systems, policies, practices, and mechanisms. It should demonstrate that kind of support. But success relies on each person internalizing that feeling of being valued. Managers and employees must remind themselves of the human values they stand for. The organization helps this internalization; it is then up to each person to keep it in mind while working with others.

There are many ways to help clients in the pursuit of the unmeasurably important:

- Legitimize the discussion of vision and values by discussing them yourself. Explore with individuals what they want to get out of their lives through their work.

Talk about how this relates to what is happening in the company right now.

- Collect data from individuals on their vision and values; bring these data to their group for discussion.
- Suggest that groups set aside time to talk about matters that are important to them but that they seldom discuss and that are not quantifiable. Do not expect that time to just appear. It won't; it must be created.
- Provide a structure in which clients can talk about their vision and values, a structure that starts where they are and lets them express their own beliefs in their own ways. Expect some discomfort with this initially when they are less experienced in talking about these matters.
- Encourage them to get away from the office to a relaxing, different setting where they are likely to relate to each other differently.
- Help them return to the important unmeasurable messages again and again so that they will be more likely to understand, believe, internalize, and act on them. For example, the president could carry the vision forward in all his or her messages for a year.
- Unmeasurably important points should be made consistently and differently: consistently so that others can hear the themes; differently so that the themes are expressed in a variety of ways. For example, work teams could be offered a motivation exercise (that links to a company value) for use in their regular meetings.
- People respond when they hear stories that support the core values of the company. See to it that the stories are collected and told at important occasions. For example, tell new employees the stories while they are learning about the vision and values of the company.
- Encourage people to take actions that are aligned with the company's vision. Then encourage them to tell about these actions. Write them up in the company paper.

In these ways the unmeasurable becomes tangible, pal-
pable, touchable, reachable, and real to everyone. This brings the
vision and values to reality.

Perhaps we can learn from the organized religions of the
world. They have purposes and messages that are both visionary
and value laden. They confidently offer a way of life that leads
to eternal salvation and wholeness—and they do not even have
a group of satisfied customers who come back and tell us about
their experiences! They have had considerable success over the
centuries and are experiencing a rebirth of interest in this country.
What can we in corporate and consulting life learn from them?

1. They make the message available to people on a regular basis.
   They tell us where and when we can go to hear the message
   spoken. We are confident that what we will hear is consistent
   with what we have heard before. In fact, one of the reasons
   we return to the same services is to hear words and guidance
   very much like those we heard the last time we were there.
   So their ritual and the predictability of that ritual are both
   important.
2. They attend to their membership. They carefully recruit new
   members, educate them, and provide them with a path to
   fuller membership. This too is frequently surrounded by ritual.
   They provide significant passages as members move from one
   stage to another.
3. They offer an array of activities to engage members at whatever
   level they may choose. They offer prayer services, reading pro-
   grams, religious instruction, sports, ritual ceremonies, bazaars,
   counseling, and bingo, to mention but a few. In whatever
   activities they offer, they try to appeal to their members' many
   needs, whether intellectual, spiritual, emotional, or physical.
   People can choose to engage in the community in their own
   way.
4. All religious groups link the separate parts of their work
   through a central model (read vision and values) that gives
   meaning to the parts.
5. Religious communities repeat their compelling message reli-
   giously—and in many ways. They are deeply, emotionally,
   spiritually invested in their message and they know the importance of repeating it if they are to bring it to fuller reality.

There is much to learn here as we try to help organizations create their futures. Our corporate communities also need investment of their members. And part of the meaning of participation in the corporate work is emotional and spiritual. We too need to find ways of engaging the hands, heads, and hearts of the people associated with the organization.

PART

Three

POWER & THE PARTNERSHIP

*H*ere we focus on developing a partnership with your clients—a powerful partnership in which you see each other as equals committed to a common task. Part Two, "Opening the Organization," talked about the content of the work, what consultants may be hired to do; in this part we concentrate on how we work with clients.

I will first consider the partnership, because it establishes a perspective for considering "the power" we have as consultants. The chapter on partnership contains four main elements, followed by two chapters about what you can bring to your clients to create rewarding or punishing partnerships. The chapter on power begins with more heady material about the powers we have or could have and ends with an exploration of our abuses of power, real and potential.

If you have read Parts One and Two of this book, it will come as no great surprise to you that I believe that the powers we bring spring from our deeper selves. In anticipation of the content in Chapter Eleven, I want to underline the positive aspects of personal power. Many of us wrestle with the powers that come with our work. I think this stems in part from the degree of power we see ourselves as having. Many of us see power narrowly, as primarily aggressive and selfish. Before you leap on that last statement, read more about the many powers we potentially bring to our work. Attila the Hun is only one of the power models available to us. (I will deal with variations on those darker powers in Chapter Twelve.) Understanding other approaches is empowering in itself; being able to act on them is more powerful yet.

Lingering on the horizon far beyond my description of consultant-client partnerships is an old institution central to the love in many of our lives: marriage. Though it is not mentioned specifically, you may detect that the ideal I am reaching toward in my work relationships is kin to marriage, friendship, companionship, family, and other caring arrangements between people. Earlier readings of this material on partnership drew criticism from those who believe strongly in the separation of their work from their personal relationships. I disagree, and I hope my thoughts will help some of you to take at least a tentative step closer to your clients. I want to reduce this unrealistic splitting of doing from caring in the workplace. Many of our most satisfying work accomplishments have essential others woven into their success. Pull out those people and what would remain of our excitement, our accomplishment, our meaning? This is what is behind much of what you will read in the next five chapters.

8

The Formula for a Strong Consultant-Client Partnership

*A*sk yourself these questions:

What are the key elements of a partnership with your clients? How are these elements important to you and to your clients?

I assume that you want working relationships with your clients that are healthy, balanced, and successful. Here is a "formula" for a client-consultant partnership that builds on my assumption.

Partnership is created when
the client's investment in your unique combination of
  abilities
equals
your investment in the client's unique combination of
  opportunities.

Note the balance in this definition of *partnership.* Each partner is clearly important. They need each other for the partnership to be formed, for the work to be done. This partnership emphasizes the power of both parties as given and received rather than just as wielded and taken.

Each partner must have something that the other wants. Let's use you and me as an example. If I don't have anything you want—if I don't have any money, information, expertise, love, knowledge, jewels, recognition, cars, talent, refrigerators, respect, furs, fishing trips, care, affection, attention, drugs, perspective, freedom from pain, tickets, position—if I don't have *anything* you want, then I am powerless in your eyes. I must have abilities the client wants; the client must have opportunities that I want.

The unique combination of abilities in the consultant and opportunities in the client further defines our mutual power. (We will talk more about power later. For now, see it as a positive word.) Look at that laundry list of possible wants again (money, information, expertise, love, etc.). If I have some of the things you want, but they also exist in the hands, heads, or hearts of many other people, then my power with you is reduced. And it is reduced in direct proportion to the number of other sources you have for what you want. My power with you is reduced because it is not uniquely mine. On the other hand (or head or heart), if I am one of few sources with this unique combination of powers, my power with you is increased. A client is looking for a *unique* combination of abilities; a consultant is looking for a *unique* combination of opportunities.

A partnership underscores the importance of both parties being willing to invest in their wants. It is not enough that both express their wants; action must follow for the partnership to form. You must be willing to invest effort and time, and to take risks. I must be willing to do the same. Whether we are speaking of a friendship or a client-consultant relationship, the willingness to invest is essential.

The partnership is really a psychological contract, in which the client's opportunities fit with the consultant's abilities. It can be shown like this:

The Partnership

The Client   **The Consultant**

"Here are the opportunities   "Here are the abilities I
we are willing to give you   will apply with you

_____   _____
_____   _____
_____   _____
_____   _____
_____   _____
_____   _____

if you apply these abilities   if you will give me these
with us."   opportunities."

_____   _____
_____   _____
_____   _____
_____   _____
_____   _____
_____   _____

In the next few pages we will elaborate further on the four key elements (balance, wants, unique abilities, and fit) that make the partnership work.

The Balance

*A*s a consultant, dependent on clients for my livelihood, I am especially focused on why clients choose to give power to me. From their perspective, I am a chunk of potential powers available to them, passive in my expression of those powers unless they activate me. From my perspective, they are a unique set of potential opportunities, passive in their expression of those powers unless I activate them.

I want to emphasize the mutuality of all this because I often hear consultants define themselves as being in a powerless position: "The client dangles the work in front of us; we take it or . . . we take it." I don't see us that way. I see, and act on, the balance of power that exists. I want to be a partner; I don't want to start off from a "one down" position.

Even when I know that I have the unique combination of abilities they want, I don't necessarily know whether I want to use these abilities with them. That will depend on the opportunities. Meanwhile, I am receptive to the possibility of working with them; I even encourage them to talk with me about that possibility. I must decide whether this client has the unique, worthwhile opportunities that I am looking for, while the client is deciding whether I have the unique combination of abilities that he or she is looking for. My power is increased by knowing that I have a choice.

The Wants

*R*egardless of who initiates contact, the client has the "wants." When a potential client calls, you know that he or she wants something and believes you might have it. When you or I call a potential client, we are trying to establish whether the client has a want, an opportunity, that may fit with our abilities.

What might you and I and other consultants have that clients might want? Here is a partial list:

Experience	Friendship	Support
Eyes	Vision	Contacts
Age	Ears	Authenticity
Wisdom	Information	Perspective
Accomplishment	Time	Objectivity
Values	Skill	Equipment
Products	Style	Compassion
Expertise	Guts	Credibility
Reputation	Approval	
Personality	Insight	

Yes, the list should be longer; what would you add to it? Give serious thought to this question. Your primary sources of power are on that list plus your addendum. Our definition of a partnership depends on you having *something* that those potential clients might want. Think about it. What is on your list?

So we've considered what a client might want of you. Just as important is what you might want from a client. Here is a partial list:

Money	Contract	Vision
References	Perspective	Support
Experience	Wisdom	Accomplishment
Friendship	Information	Trust
Expertise	Time	Respect
An audience	Ideas	Money
Satisfaction	Work	Compassion
Money	Risk	Authenticity

What would you add to this list? Your decisions about which work you pursue are based on the intuitive list you are already keeping. Why not make it more explicit by writing it down and prioritizing it? I'm willing to bet that you will learn something about yourself in the process.

Another point: Is it surprising that my two lists overlap? Perhaps not. There are many things that both my clients and I might want. Five are particularly important to me and, I suspect, to my clients: expertise, perspective, authenticity, friendship, and accomplishment (more about each of those later).

The Abilities

*M*y abilities must be unique enough so that clients will turn in my direction to satisfy their wants. Somehow, I must distinguish myself from other consultants. Offering what others offer, in the way others offer it, means that I get the same opportunities as everyone else. In other words, I am excluded from special opportunities for a good reason: I have nothing special to offer. I must define my uniqueness, which lies in the combination of abilities I possess.

My bias is that we should be professionally unique in personal ways. Our challenge is to find the unique combination of abilities in our work that reflects who we are as persons.

My clients have the resources to bring in any of a number of consultants who have résumés comparable to mine. Often my clients have looked closely at other consultants before choosing me, so I ask why they chose me. Their answer usually includes the concept of "fit" or "chemistry." They see my style as fitting with their own; my uniqueness fits with their uniqueness. They believe that they will be comfortable with the way I will work with them. I seldom hear, "We needed this project done by this date and you said you could do it," or "Your fees were lower than others with similar expertise," or "You had the best résumé." I interpret my clients as believing that there are plenty of consultants with the technical abilities they need; what they want is a good fit. And while they are going through those considerations, in parallel, I am doing the same. I usually am checking to see if I have the skills to do this work and am asking myself whether it is a good fit.

The Fit

*W*hat is "fit"? It has to do with being on the same wavelength; with seeing the organization in related ways; with behaving in ways that fit with the organization's norms; with respecting similar values; with working toward related, long-term goals; with reinforcing each other's contributions and comments; with respecting the way things are done in the organization; and with being mutually critical of how things are done in the organization. Fit implies more agreement than disagreement on what the problem is, what the alternatives are, and what action should be taken. Fit is supported by strong agreement on the undergirding of the project and allows room for disagreement on the project's less important elements.

As much attention as my clients pay to fit, I usually pay more. I know well how much it costs me in stress and strain to work with people or on a project where I do not feel there is a good fit. Nevertheless, it is possible for me to work with clients when there is not a good fit; I do so about 10 percent of the time. This does not spell disaster for the project; it just spells discomfort for me and my client. It is their organization; they are there full-time and I am only there part-time. They have enough problems already without having to adapt to a consultant on top of everything else. And I am used to adapting to organizations—more used to it than they are to adapting to consultants.

So far we have considered the importance of uniqueness as it relates to fit with a client. It is just as important for you to define your own uniqueness so that your work is more likely to fit with who you are. Define your professional uniqueness in a way that fits with who you are as a person. Part One of this book, "Balance and Being," offers actions to define and build on your personal uniqueness.

> *Fred struck off on his own as a consultant about eight years ago. After he had struggled to get started for about a year, a client "discovered" my friend's background and skill in getting unions decertified and used him in that capacity. Fred's success with this client led to other clients and a few articles in national publications. Today Fred is prosperous and his very successful firm of many consultants is busily engaged in breaking unions around the world. Fred's unique talent, widely requested and well paid for, has defined a special niche for him.*
>
> *Wonderful? Not so wonderful. The uniqueness that defines Fred's firm does not fit with who Fred is and what he wants to do. Have a drink with Fred and he will lament his success at doing something he really doesn't want to do. He will complain about his travel schedule. He will gripe about having to deliver one message over and over, a message he is no longer invested in. Fred successfully defined a uniqueness that is not what he really wants to stand for and do. He lives as if decertifying unions is the most important thing to him, while what is truly important goes unexplored. Fred plays a role that does not fit with who he is.*

9

What Consultants Can Bring to Clients

*W*hen I consider what I attempt to bring to clients in a unique combination, five "abilities" emerge. I am willing and able to offer:

Expertise
Perspective
Authenticity
Friendship
Accomplishment

Each is important to me in making work important to my life. In combination they define much of what I stand for as a consultant. Clients hire me because they too value these abilities.

Expertise

*C*lients usually cite my expertise as the main reason they are using me. I don't think so. Expertise is not enough of a reason for them to hire me, even though it's essential to the work they want done. I believe it's just easier to talk about expertise than about the many other unique abilities a consultant might have.

We need to have abilities the client values. We cannot get by on being ourselves and being friends; we have to be able to do something worthwhile—in the client's view. Further, that "something" must be something clients:

Cannot do because they don't know how
Cannot do because they don't have the time
Cannot do because they are not in a position to do it
Can do, although they need extra help
Can do, although they don't want to do the work

Find out which of these reasons is behind their interest in you. Their reason affects how you work with them. Their reason can make you co-designers, teacher and student, consultant and shadow consultant, or co-workers.

Clients often deal with me as if I have expertise that does not exist anywhere in the organization. That usually is not true. Most often, there are abilities hanging around the halls of the company that no one has ever bothered to gather together and put to work. I count on that being true, because if it isn't, the organization will not be able to bring about the changes it decides it wants. So from early in the consulting relationship, I am trying to put my expertise in perspective with the expertise present in the company; I do not want to build a dependence on me.

I am often assigned a level of expertise that exceeds or is different from what I actually have. Clients do this in their need for the consultant to be important—and my ego supports this because it *loves* attention. This is a long-term inflater of expertise that I have to watch out for.

Perspective

$\mathcal{F}$irst, a demonstration of perspective: Having spent my early professional years in a training department, I was disposed to think of performance problems as training problems. Especially in the realm of management behavior or interpersonal behavior, I "knew" that if someone was not doing something very well, it was because he or she didn't know how and merely needed training. And of course, I was a trainer, so wasn't that nice for both of us? Not surprisingly, now that I don't do much training anymore, I see it differently. More accurately, I see it differently now, so I don't do much training anymore. My perspective has changed. What others did for me, I now try to do for my clients.

Tom's New Perspective

> *I had been working with Tom for about two years on a variety of projects in his corporation, resulting in considerable mutual respect and trust. He began talking with me about his future in the corporation. As a result of restructuring, combined with Tom's outstanding performance, he was offered a promotion to a new position at another location. He accepted the promotion, but immediately felt very uneasy about his decision. He did not want to move. Yet he knew that within this corporation, you "always" accepted promotions. He had accepted six over the last eight years and had moved his family with every acceptance. Within his corporate work perspective, his acceptance of the promotion was the only alternative available to him—regardless of how uneasy he might feel. He felt trapped.*
>
> *One month later, Tom feels released from the trap; more than that, he feels very solid, relieved, even expansive.*

What happened? In the interim, Tom changed his perspective. He and his wife and children spent hours talking about the effect the move would have on them. Tom saw how important it is for his children to stay in their present schools with their friends. He saw and heard about the toll previous moves had taken on his wife, her life, and their relationship. They spent time thinking about how they wanted to live, envisioning the future they had together, and they put those dreams up against the reality of moving to work in another city for more money. He put his work in a life perspective and new alternatives opened to him. One of those alternatives was turning down the promotion— which is exactly what he did. He went back to management and reversed his earlier decision to take the promotion; he explained why and that he was willing to live with the consequences. Everyone was surprisingly understanding, making Tom's action easier for him. He feels terrific today because he acted in the interests of himself and his family and in the process confirmed to his family how important they are to him.

One of the most important parts of my work is bringing clients new perspectives. I help them see their world in new ways, and with their new vision, new alternatives suggest themselves. Their new views suggest actions that were literally inconceivable in the old view. Tom's example is a case in point. I am sure you have similar ones.

My point is not to exclaim with wonder at what Tom did or how I helped him. It happened because he was able to step out of his corporate perspective and into a family and life perspective. This change of perspectives opened alternatives for him and allowed choices that he simply couldn't consider when he looked at the world only as a good corporate executive. Tom did this work himself; he shifted his perspectives and actions by pursuing his own discomforts and visions. As a consultant, I helped by reinforcing what he was thinking about. I offered ideas on how he might think about his dilemma differently. I suggested ways for him to talk with his family. And I joined him in celebrating his decision. I am not suggesting that others would reach

Tom's same successful conclusion. I am saying that Tom's shift in perspective opened an important alternative to him.

I have often helped clients through the perception-shifting process in a much more active and intentional way than I did with Tom. My underlying assumption is that they probably have more skills than they are putting to use right now. What they lack, if anything, is perspective. Like all of us, they get trapped (and trap themselves) in seeing the world from only one point of view; within that viewpoint they can find few alternative actions—and none that are satisfying to them.

When they explain their problem to me, I ask lots of questions. I ask what they have tried and find that they have tried "everything." I suggest alternatives and they tell me why those alternatives "won't work." Sound familiar? They are stuck. And since they are really smart, they are really stuck! They have figured every possible angle on this and they know clearly why they cannot do anything about it except what they are doing—which is unsatisfactory.

My response to all this is *not* to say, "You need more skills to handle this." If it seems to me that skills and abilities are involved, I do some checking on the abilities they have. Most of the problems brought to me have people at the heart of them and "people" skills are required to deal with them. I find that most of my clients have many of the people skills they need to deal with the situations facing them, but that they are prevented from using these skills by a certain point of view:

- They see the situation in a way that precludes using the skills that would be appropriate to the situation.
- They don't understand that the skills might be necessary.
- They are scared to use the skills they have because of perceived consequences.
- They don't want to use their skills because they think it would be inappropriate.
- They don't know when to use their skills because no one has indicated that the skills are needed.
- They suffer in some way when they use their skills.

Each of these reasons for withholding their abilities has to do with how they see the situation. I try to help them see the situation differently in order to free them to do what they know how to do.

To get there, I start with understanding the situation as they understand it, then move to the search for other perspectives on that situation and, finally, develop alternative actions that might help them move from what they have to what they want. In the search for other perspectives, I seldom end up thinking, "They are not looking at this narrowly enough!" No, it's the different or larger or broader perspective that is useful. As we move to different, broader, wider perspectives, we move toward a life perspective. And as we move toward a life perspective—whether of an individual or an organization—we move toward empowerment and action alternatives.

Focusing on perspective rather than skill is especially useful to people with long experience in what they are doing. When we were newer to our work, we saw ourselves as learners; that legitimized the training and guidance we received. It was more likely that adding skills to our repertoire would aid our performance in those early years. Later on, it's a different story. We are more likely to perform better, and to open ourselves to alternatives, when others respect our vast knowledge and try to help us build on it.

Authenticity

I must have the opportunity to be myself while I work. Work that continually requires me to hide who I am is too burdensome to pursue at this time of my life. I can't find any good reasons to do it right now, although I can imagine needing the money so badly that it would be necessary. One of the primary reasons I do this work is that it provides me with the possibility of being myself while I am in service to others. I probably pay more attention to developing this ability than to the other four—and it is also the one where I have the most growth potential.

We consultants have the opportunity to shape a business around who we are; many other workers are asked to mold themselves to a job description, or a system, or a machine. We have a unique chance to pattern our little companies to our designs. Which leads to certain questions:

What is my design for this little business?
What is the business becoming?
What am I becoming?
Who am I in relation to my work?
Who do I want to be?
How will I present myself at work? Outside of work?
What will I tell others about who I am and what I do?

All these questions are linked to authenticity.

I believe we must be working on the answers to such questions as we venture into the marketplace. Otherwise, how do we know if who we are fits with what is needed? And how do we know what we want? We can end up being so reactive that we pass up the opportunity to define our business around our "selves." We don't need to know all the answers before venturing forth, but we do need to attempt to clarify who we are and what we want. Many answers will become clearer later in relation to what the marketplace offers—especially if we have defined what we want.

Working for yourself, by yourself, requires one helluva lot of motivation! And your motivation is directly linked to your authenticity: To the extent that through this work you are who and what you want to be, you will persevere on this path. To the extent that this work requires that you play a role that doesn't fit you, the path will be less attractive and you will be less motivated.

The basic reason to pursue authenticity in your work is not so that you will be motivated; that is just a valuable by-product. The better reason is that there is nothing more important to do in this life than becoming yourself. And you can do that by being an authentic consultant. When you intend to become yourself through your work, a lot of complications are eliminated:

You don't have to remember what role you are trying to play, because you are being yourself. You can forget about how you should behave at work and at home because there is no difference in the perspective you bring to each place; the differences are in the situation. You don't have to tell small lies in order to cause people to think you are someone you are not. You don't have to pretend, invent, fake, or feign interest. There is nothing to make up; there is no posturing to do. Your life is simplified by your authenticity.

How easily I am seduced
By my public caring, charity,
thoughtfulness.
Fooling myself for awhile,
Letting myself believe
That these are selfless acts
While I bask in the affection
of friends.

I recently discovered a gap in my authenticity while doing some volunteer consulting work. I found myself being unusually blunt with the client group. And my bluntness was unusually effective, partly because it was so clear. I later realized that I was behaving differently because I was not being paid to do the work. Hmmm. I learned something about what I withhold from my paying clients, for fear of losing their friendship, the work, and my reputation. My success with the volunteer work caused me to think that I may also be withholding my effectiveness from paying clients. That experience moved me a notch closer to authenticity with other clients.

Friendship

*P*ut aside your role as a consultant for a minute and think about what you want from and with your friends. Put this book down and mentally list a handful of statements, each beginning with, "I want . . . ." When you have collected your wants, read those I have listed:

- I want to be myself (there is authenticity again) and I want people to accept me as I am.
- I want my friends to tell me why they like me, as well as how I get on their nerves.
- I want to be able to do risky, even silly, things with my friends, knowing that they will accept my behavior.
- I want to be able to talk about what is important to me and to be taken seriously.

- I want to work and play with friends, accomplish things, reach goals shoulder to shoulder, and enjoy together those accomplishments.
- I want to be able to talk with friends about my concerns, knowing that they will support me.
- I want my friends to be comfortable with me, to talk, to take risks, to share concerns, to be serious, and generally to want to work and play with me.

My bet is that much of what I want with friends you also want. Our lists are probably close enough so that you will understand when I say that my ideal client partnerships are friendships.

When I meet with a potential client, I am thinking about friendship and I evaluate that possibility. It is not necessary for me to be friends with all of my clients, but when it happens it certainly adds to the authenticity and enjoyment in my work. When I think back on the work I have been proudest of, learned the most from, and contributed the most in, 80 percent of the time friendship was involved. And the friendship contributed to the positive results.

Now here's the tough part: When I think about the work that I didn't enjoy, didn't learn from, or didn't contribute much to, some of the time (30 percent?) friendship was also involved. Friendship with clients does not guarantee success; in fact, it can complicate matters significantly. But it is so positive when it is present that it offsets the complications that can come with it. I would rather live with those occasional complications than deprive myself of the richness that is added to my work by my client-friends. I spend many hours of my life devoted to this work; I see no important reason for not seeking friends through my work.

Coincidentally, while I was writing this section, I received a telephone call from an old client-friend. We have worked together in three different organizations over the last eight years. I hadn't heard from him for about two years. He called because he was reading my first book, thinking of me, and wondering how I was doing. We chatted for twenty minutes about our work and our families, and enjoyed catching up. One of the things we talked about is this section on friendship that you are reading right now. His call came because we became friends through our work together.

I am reminded of the dated guidance many of us received when we moved into a supervisory position—something to the effect that as a supervisor you must be careful about being too friendly with your employees. They will take advantage of you, or you will not be able to be objective, or life will just get too complicated. All of those concerns are valid, but they are diminished by the rich potential of combining work and personal relationships. As a manager, and now as a consultant, I have found the risk small compared to the rewards.

Pursuit of friendships is just one more example of seeing consulting as a path toward meaning in life. Friends are an important part of my life; work is an important part of my life. Friendships are built by doing things with people; therefore, why not have friends at work?

The possibility of developing friendships with these partners-in-work affects how you deal with them:

- It guides you toward openness, equality, naturalness, and authenticity.
- It causes you to look for opportunities to be with them and to do things with them, beyond just work.
- It means that you end up talking with them at all hours of the day and night.
- It makes it difficult to sort work from nonwork. You get involved in each others' families, hear about what is going on at home, or find yourselves at each others' family celebrations.

Being friends with my clients takes away some things that are at least occasionally important to me:

- I miss being set apart, being treated as special. As I become "one of the crowd," people forget that I am the expert.
- People begin to wonder why they are paying me so much money when I am so ordinary, not much different from them.
- I lose my objectivity as I get close to the issues of the organization. As I work there longer, I become more a part of the issues, and less an observer of them.

- If people become familiar enough, they call me at home to talk about work and personal problems, and this cuts into other personal time.
- I lose the ability to control my professional image of being highly knowledgeable, always having good ideas, and knowing what to do next.

So there are losses as the clients find out who I really am—and most of what is lost is pretense and image.

My clients say that they are not used to having consultants treat them as friends. They like the way I work with them and see it as unusual. (Of course, the ones who do not like it do not work with me; they have found a consultant who fits with what they do like.) My approach to them sets me apart in positive ways. They tell me that it makes me unique. From a marketing perspective, what a wonderful side effect of this life pursuit!

Accomplishment

*A*ccomplishment is achieving results about which both you and your client can say, "This worked!" We have all done work that our clients were happy with, but that we were unhappy with. Imagine that this is a pattern and you have one definition of an ineffective client-consultant relationship. As the consultant, I also must get something out of this. I am not doing this work just to make clients happy; I want to be happy too!

Accomplishment can be realized at a number of levels: a successful meeting today, a successful project next month, a successful strategic accomplishment three years from now. What is important is that accomplishments at all levels are both realized and recognized. Sometimes they must be pointed out and emphasized: "Look at what we have done together today," or "I feel proud of what we have accomplished over the last year," or "You people have done one terrific job of bringing this dream to reality!"

I emphasize accomplishment for two reasons. First, I love to help clients get things done! That is part of the excitement for me about being a consultant, so I want to celebrate with them when we make progress. Second, I think clients pay more attention to accomplishment than to any of the other elements (perspective, authenticity, expertise, and friendship) of the client-consultant partnership—and they ought to! Our meeting and contracting to do work is based on the assumption of some valued contribution from me. I may be as authentic as hell, have expertise running out of my attaché case, provide them with forty-seven perspectives, and be the best friend they could ever have, but if we don't get something done together, our work is in trouble!

Another word on accomplishment: Build patterns of accomplishment. Starting with small successes (like a good meeting) attend to what you and the client accomplish together. Talk about your accomplishments; don't take them for granted. On long projects, you will probably have setbacks, and it is nice to be able to place these setbacks in some perspective with an established pattern of accomplishment in your partner's mind.

Try to be aware of how you contributed within the accomplishment. This is not always easy to identify, but it has a great deal to do with why you are working for this client. Your sense of your contribution can help you to decide how much you should participate in the next steps on a project. For example, if your recent contributions have been minimal, if your presence didn't really make that much difference, this could suggest that the client is ready to work without you. Or it could suggest that if you are to be important to this project, you had better find some new ways of contributing.

Clients often need help in recognizing what they have accomplished—for at least two reasons. First, you may have helped them do something they have never done before, so when it happens they are not experienced enough to recognize what they have accomplished. Second, they are so busy producing and solving problems that they may not stop to look back at their progress. Helping our client-partners celebrate what they have done brings new learning and new energy to the work we are doing together. It helps all of us recognize that we are moving forward.

I recently met with a client middle-management group to discuss progress on a project we have been pursuing together for the last six months. Before the meeting, cafeteria conversation centered around how little had actually been accomplished, despite a major effort in the plant. Early in the meeting, the plant manager asked small groups to list what had happened in the plant since the start of this major effort and because of it. Fairly soon the groups were buzzing with discussion; after twenty minutes they had listed over five pages of actions they would attribute to this major effort. We were all amazed at what had been accomplished so far.

Building Trust and Willingness to Risk

W hat does it cost a client to benefit from this unique combination of abilities that you offer? By "cost," I am not referring just to money. And is it worth it? By "worth it," I am not referring just to quantifiable results. Anticipating the answers to these questions causes the client to move toward or away from you. No matter how able and unique you may be, at decision time the client will decide whether it is worth it to invest in you.

This potential investment for the client contains many elements; the tangible, measurable, or quantitative elements are usually not the most important. There is a cost/benefit ratio at work that is usually more subjective than objective. There are opportunities and risks in

The way the project is defined
How you are used in the company
Exposing yourself to higher management
Defining issues in the organization
Raising expectation levels

The clients are aware that this consulting intervention could benefit or cost in ways much more important than money. Besides dollars, they will be spending a lot of time. They risk moving in directions as yet undefined based on information as yet uncollected. They are deeply invested in their own and the organization's success. They are considering putting some portion of this potential success on the line with you, a consultant. They are considering giving you powers in their organization that they ordinarily reserve for themselves and a few trusted others. They know that things will be different after you begin work and that all of those differences are not predictable. They must ask themselves if this is a smart investment.

Words going through the client's mind at this time might include trust, risk, control, trust, opportunity, risk, trust, concern, excitement, trust—and maybe risk. The most important elements in this investment decision are the nonquantifiable, intangible, and subjective elements that build trust, based on the support found in your unique combination of abilities. (We will talk more about trust in a few pages.) Thoughtful clients are not going to hire you to do important work if they do not sense a good fit.

The considerations in hiring a consultant are very similar to the decisions the client makes when hiring full-time staff. Candidates are checked out for the resources and powers that they bring. Their talents, abilities, and style allow their uniqueness to show, which selects them in or out of the process. The employer looks through the better applicants for fit and generally uses this to decide. The potential employee is going through the same process. A major difference in the client-consultant process is that we consultants go through the "employment process" repeatedly every year. And we are being considered for a relatively short period of "employment." Our repeated experiences with getting "hired" can aid us in learning how to make the process go well for us and our clients.

While the client is deciding whether to invest in me, I'm considering my part of the partnership. The client must have an opportunity that I want to invest in. It must be a unique opportunity, where I can see a real possibility of contributing. For the partnership to work, there must be a long-term balance of powers between us that respects the organization and my occasional presence in it. My power comes partly from the fact that I will not be here for long. The client gives me the opportunity to work here, knowing that I will leave. And the client knows that he or she is in charge. All the powers that I have are balanced out by the power the client holds to choose me or not.

While I am writing this, the shadowy image of high school dances comes to mind. I see girls talking with each other along one wall and a crowd of boys a safe distance away. The music is playing, and for those who want to dance, this is the moment. (In my school, the girls waited to be asked by the boys, or danced with each other.) The boys are

> *clearly in a powerful position. A boy glances across the room, figuring out which girl he would like to dance with or, if he knows, trying to work up the nerve to ask. After deciding which girl is most qualified for this opportunity to be his partner, he strolls across the floor to ask her to dance. As he moves across the floor, the balance of power shifts. A moment ago, he held the power to choose; now she has the power to accept or reject him.*

As discussed earlier, the client-consultant partnership is going to be based on a good fit between the two. Trust and risk are key elements in creating that fit. Before describing them, know that each must be mutual for the partnership to work well. Both partners must trust; both must risk. Another point: Trust and risk operate in relation to each other. Movement in one affects the other. How they affect each other is not as predictable as the fact that they will.

Here are some things I've observed about trust and risk with clients.

- A client's trust of me increases his or her willingness to risk with me, and vice versa.
- It is pointless for me to encourage a client to risk if he or she does not yet trust me.
- A client who is willing to risk a great deal—out of proportion to the relationship we have established—is likely to be desperate, foolish, thoughtless, or very brave.
- A client who apparently trusts me—out of proportion to the relationship we have established—is likely to be desperate, foolish, ignorant, or very insightful.
- A pattern of resistance from clients about the size, costs, timing, or any other factual details of the project indicates lack of trust or unwillingness to risk.
- A client's unwillingness to risk can be related to trusting me or to perceptions of what is happening in the organization. Both deserve attention. The former is easier to act on because I am part of the difficulty. It must be dealt with first to allow significant work on the latter.

This short list is guidance for thought, rather than action. In other words, think about it and test it before acting on it. Clients' feelings about trust and risk are influenced by many factors that we don't control—from factors inside the organization to those buried in childhood. In much consulting, there is nothing that can reduce the real risk present in the work. By building trust, however, I often can make the risk more acceptable.

So, what can you do to support clients' willingness to take risks and to increase their trust? Much of the following list will be specific elaboration on the expertise, perspective, authenticity, friendship, and accomplishment abilities discussed earlier:

- Provide information willingly and openly about yourself.
- Initially, encourage clients to talk with other clients you have worked with.
- Explain related projects you have completed, going into some detail to assure them that you know what you are doing.
- Learn about and understand their organization as they understand it. Be able to tell them how you see them thinking and feeling about it.
- Show your respect for the organization and what the clients are trying to accomplish in it. Study what they have done successfully and talk with them about why it worked.
- Work in ways that respect and honor the culture of the organization. If the clients work long hours, you work long hours. Demonstrate your belief in them and the business.
- Point out how you are trying to help them accomplish their ends. Make their goals your goals—and remind them regularly that this is true.
- When you see risky situations, point them out. Help clients deal with the risks they face. Help them see you as a resource that will help them through risky times.
- Model risk taking. Show them that you too are willing to risk to serve their ends.
- Voice doubts and fears, as well as hopes and joys. Demonstrate that you are not fearless, just as they are not.

- Make commitments and follow through on them. Show them that you truly want something to happen—and that what you want fits with what they want.
- Find opportunities to take actions that demonstrate your support of what you are all working toward. Words only go so far.
- Be with clients the way you want them to be with you. If you want more openness, then be open. If you want them to listen, then listen more yourself.
- Share responsibility for getting work done. Holding it all to yourself encourages the opposite of trusting and risking.

10

Rewarding and Punishing Partnerships

 To conclude this partnership discussion, I thought back over partnerships that have been more and less effective for me. I added the thoughts of some friends (*through a discussion led by Mac McCullough in the Woodlands Group*) and came up with two lists. It's the "good news/bad news" of partnerships.

I suggest that before reading my lists, you jot down a few notes to yourself. What have been the high and low spots of your relationships with clients? What patterns do you see in your highs or your lows? Doing this resulted in new discoveries for me, and perhaps will for you.

Creating Frustration and Failure

$\mathcal{P}$unishing partnerships can be caused by the following factors:

The contracting is unclear.   We find partway down the road that we are trying to do different things from those we contracted to do. Or we build a plan with difficulty based on two different sets of assumptions. Or we talk about outcomes, but never discuss underlying values. In other words, we really do not know what we are going to do together, how we are going to do it, or why it is important. But we think we know.

I work my agenda, not the client's.   I "knew better" coming into the situation. I didn't bother to give the client company what it wanted; instead, I gave it what I knew it needed. I have done this at least three times that I can recall. In every case the work had positive outcomes—and I was not invited back to do more work. Somehow in the process I lost sight of who was sponsoring me and the need for me to honor their wants.

There is poor personal fit between us.   As important as fit is to me, I find myself accepting work that looks interesting and trying to put aside the weak relationship between me and my partner. An example: Two years ago I was pursued by someone who wanted me to work for his company. I say "pursued" because I took an immediate dislike to him and tried politely to avoid the opportunity to work with him. He explained the work to me and the work itself sounded interesting. I began to rationalize. Perhaps by charging more money than usual I could get over the problems I would have dealing with him, or be compensated for the extra trouble. I accepted the work at a higher rate and suffered through it. I was wrong; it wasn't worth it. And it was my mistake, not his. There is just no point in encouraging people to use me when I don't want to work with them.

The client has financial constraints narrower than the work to be done.   Trying to operate within too tight financial boundaries dampens the whole project. None of us feels free to think expansively. When I take on such confined work, I spend more time on the project than I get paid for, and I end up resenting the client because I decided to take on the work. Sometimes clients will sense this; sometimes I tell them—which complicates our dynamics and takes even more time that I am not paid for.

The project becomes less important to the client than it is to me.   After a decent beginning, the project starts slipping off track. The track is constantly changed. Meetings are rescheduled. I am kept waiting. The client ends up paying me to sit around and wait. All of these are symptoms of slippage. In retrospect, I can see the seeds of this slippage planted as far back as our initial contracting. My responsibility is to tell the client what I see happening and what I interpret it to mean, and to get the client's response.

I accept work that is outside my primary expertise.   I occasionally do this during a bout of financial anxiety. As a matter of fact, that is probably why I will do it again in the future! But the underlying reason for accepting the wrong kind of work is that I allow myself to be seduced. The prospective clients mention nice things they have heard about my work; while I am drooling, they suggest that it would be nice to work together sometime, and I nod yes. Later they call, remind me of how wonderful they think my work is, and suggest that we meet to talk about a project they are working on. We do that and I try to be wonderful. In the process I agree to work with them on a project that doesn't really fit with what I want to do. It's not their fault that I choose to do this. Hmmmmm . . . must be mine.

I work for the money.   One of the worst reasons I can think of to take on work is for the money. If that is the main reason I am working for this client, the chances are that I will find the work a struggle. I used to do this more often; even this year I have had a time or two when I looked at my calendar and got nervous about the blank spots in it. Then somebody called and got immediate favorable consideration because I was nervous about my bank account. I don't like it when money gets in the way of work; worrying about the financial side of the work is a distraction from the main point. I should be asking myself whether I believe I can do this work for them successfully, not whether I need the money. (This is addressed further in Part Four, "Money and the Marketplace.")

I catch the "disease."   Sometimes, when working with clients, I get so close to the issues, and become so much a part of the culture, that I end up becoming part of the problem. Whatever the "illnesses" are that afflict this organization begin to show up in me. I begin behaving in the same less-effective ways that they are. We begin to talk about it. Then the clients end up paying me to solve problems they have with me while I am trying to help them with problems they have with each other. It gets very complicated and I don't feel very good about the work. I usually feel worse about this than the client does, partly because I am more aware of having "caught something." The illness metaphor seems particularly appropriate; when this happens to me it really is like catching the flu or a cold.

> *In the midst of a large project with an insurance company, a design team and I were working on an identified problem: People in the organization were highly averse to taking risks. The reasons were many, including fear of losing their jobs, fear of the key executives, and fear of rejection after good ideas had been stomped on in the past. You get the idea. Our planning to put this issue before the organization took one meeting, then two meetings, then three. I began to get very uncomfortable. We just couldn't seem to get together an approach that was supported by the planning team. We found ourselves bound up in details and trying to provide for every possibility. I wasn't being very helpful, and I wasn't talking to the team about my discomfort, figuring that since we were already spending too much time on this, we shouldn't spend even more on my problems. It was about then that I figured it out: I had caught the disease. The reason we couldn't put a plan together was that*

we *were afraid of getting fired,* we *were afraid of the key executives,* we *were afraid our good ideas would be rejected. Our issues weren't out there in the organization; they were in here, in this team, in us, in me. I was, in effect, supporting their risk-avoidance behaviors. My actions reinforced the idea that this was a fearful place to work, it's those people out there we have to watch out for, and we can't do a lot about it. That wasn't very helpful.*

I am more aware of my susceptibility to others' maladies now, but I have not developed an immunity or found a booster shot that protects me. Catching the disease still screws up my work.

I have naïve positive assumptions about the abilities of people in the organization. Ordinarily my positive assumptions about people serve me well, but often I expect someone to deliver on something he or she is just not prepared to do. I deal with these people as if they can handle it; I don't make it easy for them to say, "I don't know how," or "I need help." When their piece of the work runs aground, special effort is needed to help them. It often would have taken less effort to prepare them well in the first place, and at less cost to the larger project. These naïve assumptions also include supporting the wrong people for key player roles—for example, that of my internal counterpart. When the internal consultant cannot guide the project effectively, the project is in trouble and I am in trouble. Recognizing my pattern of naïve positive assumptions has moved me toward more consciously assessing the skills of the people I am working with.

I maintain a pretense. There is something going on here that the client is not talking about. There is something going on here that I am not talking about. And it is important. I suspect that the client and I both know that we are avoiding talking about it. We are acting as if it is not there— whatever it is. In my case, I am usually fooling myself by maintaining that it is not very important and that we are focused on the key issues.

I worked with the executive committee of a company in the computer industry. The work involved redefining the company's mission and direction, supporting it with a change strategy that (eventually) required everyone in the company to look at the company's mission, direction, philosophy, and values. The CEO of the company was sleeping with the vice-president of finance. Yes, they are of opposite sexes, and yes, one of them was married. Everybody knew it and, further, believed that the VP was being favored at work. This was in direct conflict with the company's newly espoused values but no one was talking with the CEO and VP about it. As a result, when the CEO talked to groups about the company's direction and values, it was not very believable. His relationship with the VP was undermining important company efforts. And everyone, including me, was pretending.

That is a dramatic example of the pretenses we can get caught up in. We were all pretending that we did not know about their affair. I found myself pretending for a while, but I am better at noticing my own pretense than I used to be. Once I became aware of it, I had to figure out what to do about it.

Postscript: After talking with a few people, I talked with the CEO. I stopped pretending and told him what was being discussed in the organization as well as how his behavior was being linked to company values by the people who worked for him. I told him this so he could act on this new knowledge. I continued to work with him for at least another year. We never discussed it again, though he alluded to our discussion once. And what happened between him and the vice-president? I don't know. I do know that they had the information about how their relationship affected the organization, and they knew that others knew.

Building Satisfaction and Success

*R*ewarding partnerships can be caused by the following factors:

We have a shared vision of where the work is leading. That vision guides our day-to-day decisions and is always more important than the plans or procedures we put in place to accomplish the vision. Our work is something of a pioneering effort. We're heading for the mountains in the far distance, and deserts, rivers, and forests must be crossed to get there.

Our work is important to us and to others. The larger the circle of "investors," the better. For example, working with a hospital management team has a positive potential for the team, but also for the patients, the employees, the community, the insurers, and the medical profession as a whole. If the client has a boss, that boss supports the project and follows its progress.

We define and work within a structure that serves our purposes. We have a plan or model that we honor as we decide what happens next in the project. For example, I helped an executive committee develop a strategic planning process. Over the next two years, they did their planning within that process. Along the way, they learned more about planning, what worked and what didn't. They modified their process accordingly. Annual planning sessions always included a look into how the process was working.

We deliver results—not just activity—from our work together. Each contact is intended to produce results that contribute to our larger plan or model. We know what we are going to do today and how it will move us forward.

We talk frequently during the project. Information is exchanged in both directions. We talk about what is working well and what is not. We have mutual confidence that we will keep each other current on what is happening. We feel free to call each other at any time, days, nights, or weekends, but we respect each other's need for work and life outside this project.

We see each other as partners. We both expect to work, contribute, make mistakes, and succeed together. There is a mutual acknowledgment that we are learning from doing this work together. We are each experienced and neither of us knows it all. We are willing to explore, take risks, and be innovative.

Getting the work done is more important than sticking to our roles. We see defined roles as useful starting points in our understanding of each other, rather than as absolute definitions of who we are or how we will work. We are willing to put aside our roles to do what the situation requires. For example, I expect that the client will sometimes be the consultant and occasionally I will act more like a client.

There is a personal fit between us. We can converse easily. The understanding between us goes beyond what has been said. We find each other interesting. There is the possibility of a friendship that could be more important than the work.

Clients know that because it is their organization, they will have to do the most important work. Better yet, they want to do the work. They see me best used as an adviser, guide, helper, and coach. They know that if the project is to succeed, it cannot be done *for* them.

I have a solid working relationship with an internal counterpart in the client's organization. A good counterpart is competent, trusted, and organizationally well placed to work on this project. This person does not need to have my expertise, though that can be helpful. He or she carries the day-to-day responsibility for the project; we work together as a team.

11

The Powers of the Consultant

*P*ower is variously defined as the ability to:

Choose
Act
Influence others
Control others
Cause others to act
Make happen what you want to happen
Get what you want

A definition I prefer is:

Power is knowing what you want and acting upon it.

I like the accent on self-knowledge as being essential to powerful action. (*Jim Maselko helped me with these thoughts years ago.*) I like the responsibility this definition gives to me. Yes, it can be seen as being self-centered and disregarding others. But because the goodwill of others is so central to what I want, my potential to abuse personal power is tempered.

Some of my underlying assumptions about power are no doubt evident if you have read this far. But let's elaborate on them:

Power is essential for life.
Power is a potentially positive, as well as negative, force.
Power is available to and important to everyone.
Power exists in relationship to others.

I intentionally begin this chapter on power with a positive emphasis because of the negative connotations power has developed over the years. All its abuses have caused me to hesitate to say that I am powerful or that I want power. Seeking power or taking powerful actions is often associated with selfishness and harshness, and that is not a part of me I like to acknowledge publicly.

I must admit that I can find that darker power lurking in my personal shadows. That power is more coercive in its intent. It is autocratic and controlling, showing little respect for the contributions of others. By closing itself off from others, it "knows better than." It intentionally precludes knowledge, intentionally narrows learning. That power exists in me and occasionally I exercise it.

But here we will focus on how power is essential, positive, available, and important to our relationships with our clients. We must be powerful to be successful. I mention this early because I often sense consultants' aversion to power. They don't like thinking of themselves as power-wielding people. I struggle with this too, but I also know I want to make a difference—to accomplish something—and that takes power.

For the next few pages think of power as all those positive alternatives that allow you to get things done. After exploring positive uses of our power, we will look at some of the real and potential abuses of the power that comes with consulting.

Sources of Consulting Power

*V*arious experts have categorized the kinds of power at work that are available to members of an organization. Often they come down to six categories; here are those six. (*I have adapted these from Pamela Cuming's* The Power Handbook.) As you read through them, think about which powers are most available to and effective for consultants with long-term clients:

Power of authority.   You are a powerful person because the organization has put you in a position of responsibility. You make decisions that others are expected to honor. Your position has been formally defined and is more permanent than temporary.

Power of reward.   You have favors (money, gifts, goodies, help, recognition) you can bestow on people when you like what they do. People want these rewards and will perform differently in order to gain your favors.

Power of punishment.   You can punish people and get away with it. You can hurt them or coerce them and they know it. They will behave differently in order to avoid the penalty of running afoul of you.

Power of association.   Over the years you have built a network of good connections with people in high places. You know a lot of people who are important to the work at hand. People treat you as special because of your connections with these other powerful people. You maintain your contacts and others know it.

Power of expertise.   Your power comes from all of the knowledge, skill, experience, and ability you have accumulated in your field. People come to you for help because they want to use your talent.

Power of relationship.   You have power with people because you have a positive personal connection with them. They have a caring or affection for you that you can build upon, and vice versa. You trust each other because of this relationship.

As consultants, which powers can we use regularly with our clients? I believe we can use them all but should cultivate a few—namely, expertise and relationship. Before talking about them, let me say why I don't see the other four as primary sources of power for consultants.

Authority.   We seldom have legitimate power that compares to similar powers in the organization. Our power of position is temporary and does not command the same respect (or obedience) that others in authority have. We cannot count on having this power, so we cannot build our power base upon it.

Reward.   We do have rewards we can give others. We can recognize their contributions to the project; we can give our time and attention to them as a reward for their efforts. We should use this power but not plan on it being a primary power source.

Punishment.   Here is a source of power we have and should avoid using. Our information about the organization and its members is privileged. When we use that information to punish people, we jeopardize our standing in the organization. We should be clear with people how we will use what we know and that clarity should encourage trust, not suspicion or fear.

Association.   Our contacts should be used carefully. Though our contacts with others may be an aid, we are better off building on the power that comes directly from us, rather than indirectly from others.

So for many reasons, the "winners" are the powers of expertise and relationship.

Expertise. Expertise gets us in the door. It justifies our presence. We cannot be powerful in any lasting way without bringing skills, experience, perspective, knowledge, or something else that adds to what the client already possesses.

Relationship. Given the importance of risk taking in bringing about change in client organizations, trust of the consultant is extremely important. That trust is less likely to exist without a positive personal relationship between us and our clients. It is important, and often essential, that we build on the power of relationship.

These two powers in combination provide the foundation of long-term, effective client-consultant partnerships. These are the two we should cultivate. The other four powers are not to go neglected and unused, but can be used to supplement expertise and relationship.

Perceptions as Power

- If you have expertise in an area but do not recognize it, your power is diminished.
- If you have expertise but your potential clients do not know it, your power is diminished.
- If neither you nor they recognize the power of your expertise, you might as well not have it, even if you really do!
- If you perceive that you have expertise, your power is increased, in the sense that you will be more likely to initiate, involve yourself, and see yourself as a legitimate player.
- If your expertise is only self-perceived and not real, your power is likely to come to an untidy and embarrassing end, but before that happens, you will act as though you know what you are talking about simply because you believe you do. And there is power in that: You act in more powerful ways when you believe you have expertise.

- If you perceive that you do not have expertise, your power is diminished. Even if you really have it, you will have less power because you believe you do not have it. In fact, you (with the expertise but not perceiving it) might meet with me (with the perception of expertise but without the reality). In our meeting, power is likely to flow in my direction on the basis of our mutual misperceptions.
- If I perceive that you have expertise, your power is increased. Whether you've got it or not is not the point here; if I think you've got it, I treat you as if you have, and that increases your power with me. And conversely . . .
- If I perceive that you do not have expertise, your power is decreased with me. No matter how smart you may be on the subject, if I don't believe it you are less powerful with me.

Imagine what happens when reality and perception on your part and my part are wrapped up in a client-consultant relationship. It gets very complicated. It *is* very complicated! Even if we confine ourselves to the power of expertise, as we did in the eight preceding statements, there are many possible permutations between us. If you add others to our group, the variations expand geometrically. And if you move beyond expertise to other powers, it becomes more complicated still. Such an interplay of power realities and perceptions is going on that it is impractical to attempt to track them objectively. In fact, we all track them subjectively, intuitively, as we interact with each other.

Managing Our Power

*S*ee the powers we have been discussing as sources of your strength. Assume that people, clients, are drawn to your strength. They want to tap that power and effectiveness. Your power with the client is well established. Now, how are you going to use it?

I am imagining ourselves as hydrants with power hoses connected to them, hoses of various sizes, hydrants of various colors. Each hydrant and hose is ready to deliver the power stored behind it at whatever rate we choose to release it. The power supply is not inexhaustible, but it is considerable and reliable. Now, in the face of a "fire," how do we use the powers available to us? In what combination? With what intensity? For how long? In which directions? After building our power, our challenge as consultants is to maintain it by using it well.

Clients have a way of elevating consultants to power pedestals. This reduces our effectiveness in their organizations. They want us to have the answers to their questions and the solutions to their problems. Too often we try to meet those needs by taking responsibility for giving all the right answers and finding all the best solutions. We feed their dependence on us and in the process weaken them. To steal a profound thought from Confucius, we feed them a fish a day rather than teaching them how to fish. We forget whose organization it is and who needs to be responsible. As we do this, we participate in elevating our power inappropriately in the organization.

Though I see consultants primarily as guides who help clients to use their own resources better, the fact is that we do occasionally have a useful answer or solution. That truth complicates our exercise of power. It would be much cleaner if we were always in a helping and support role, but we are not— at least, I am not. (For more on this, see "Facilitating Is Not Enough," in Chapter Three.) Our experience reinforces our opinions. Hours of work in a system develop our biases about what ought to be done. Listening to the client work out alternatives stimulates alternatives in our own minds. When we bring our opinions, biases, and alternatives forward, we step out of the background into the foreground, and our role has changed. So has our exercise of power.

We often bring expertise that is very relevant to the content of the meeting and that takes us out of the observing and processing role. For example, with research and experience, I know a great deal about strategic planning, and I am qualified to offer direction on what they plan, not just observations on how they are working together. Through experience and writing, I know a lot about leadership, and I am comfortable showing clients effective ways to lead. I also know something about decision making. Launching forth with any of this content in mind does make me more of a player than an observer. I become responsible in new ways: I invest myself in a position; I care about the content that is being discussed. And this is likely to make my role to the group (and myself) more complicated, even if it is valued.

These power dilemmas require that we know which hat we are wearing (player or sideline commentator or coach or cheerleader or spectator) at the moment, and that we attend to how we put our contributions forward. Here is some guidance that I have found useful:

- When contracting with clients, I tell them how I see my role. I include in that role the option of putting forth my own ideas on the content they are working with. And I ask them to listen to my ideas as they would listen to each others'. I try to do this near the beginning of our working relationship, and then remind them of this aspect of my role when it seems important—for example, at the beginning of an important meeting that I am facilitating.

- I tell clients I am aware that I am now offering ideas that lie in a realm outside my primary expertise. (In other words, I may not know what I'm talking about!) My reminder to them is not because they may have forgotten, but so they will know that I have not forgotten.

- Before offering content-related thoughts, I check with myself to make sure that the ideas do not come out of my ignorance. This double-checking does not always work, but it does keep me from getting in the way of their discussion.

- I am careful about asking content questions when I am the only one in the room who needs the answer. The client's job is not to educate me. I don't want to waste other people's time while I increase my expertise on the content of their discussion.

This guidance helps me, and may help you, but it does not resolve the power dilemma. Sharing the dilemma with the client is a first step toward managing it.

Powerful Actions

*T*here are a number of useful actions you can take to explore your power sources.

1. Ask yourself, "What do I have as a consultant that would allow clients and potential clients to give power to me?" Look again at the list of wants in Chapter Eight and note powers that you recognize as actually having now. Add to the list any other powers that come to mind.

2. Elaborate on the powers you noted in item 1. Write a paragraph to yourself about each of them. Tell yourself about your expertise, your perspective, your time, or whatever your power source might be.

3. Incorporate elements of your self-description from item 2 in the way you talk about yourself professionally. Find ways of giving appropriate expression to your power so that others can see that power in you.

4. List the powers you think others—especially clients—attribute to you. Turn off any thoughts about whether you agree or disagree with those powers; just list them. Look at the relationship of this list to what you attribute to yourself:

   • Where do you have knowledge (or at least perceptions) of powers that your clients lack?
   • Where do you suspect that they give you powers that you do not give yourself?
   • What can you do about these differences?
   • What do you want to do about these differences?

5. Find out in what ways clients see you as powerful. Do this in a way that excludes your influence as much as possible. Ask them to talk among themselves about what makes you more and less effective (powerful) with them. Leave the room and have them take notes. Or distribute a questionnaire that reviews the work you have done and that includes some power-related questions. Or have a heart-to-heart talk with a client with whom you work especially well. Ask a few power-related questions, sit, be quiet, and listen. Your intent is to see how others see your power, not for you to lead them toward your perceptions or away from their own.

6. Talk with your friends (not your clients) about what makes you powerful in their lives. If your personal and professional lives are congruent, then most (maybe all) of the powers that your friends attribute to you can be transferred to your work as a consultant. Some of them might need a little translating in the process, but they will have their place. This is based on my belief that we will be better consultants to the extent that we are true to ourselves in our professional work.

7. Ask your friends how they think you fool yourself in your approach to your life and your work. For example, how do you diminish yourself by holding a perception of yourself that is less powerful than the reality of who you are? How do you elevate yourself inappropriately by holding a self-perception that is grander than the reality?

12

The Darker Side of Consultants' Power

Abuses of Power

*I*t is important to acknowledge the darker side of the power spectrum within ourselves. Denying it blinds us to its presence and strength. If we haven't looked at it, it is hard to recognize when it shows up in our work. Here are some examples of power abuses I have been tempted by in my work:

- Giving a client confidential information in ways that violate the conditions under which the information was gathered—in order to support directions in which I think the organization should move
- "Selling" a specific action, using the power of the consultant position to convince client managers that what I want is best for them—and doing this in such a way that other alternatives do not get a fair hearing
- Aligning myself with the president of the company against the vice-presidents on the management committee, supporting his or her position and seeing to it that their input gets less consideration—when the management committee is supposed to be my client
- Distorting data I have gathered so that the problems of the organization are more evident—since "I know" what problems deserve to be worked on
- Undermining someone I see as an ineffective manager by making an opportunity to pass on negative information to her or his boss and by dwelling on it in a way that makes that manager a problem in the boss's mind
- Behaving as if I understand more about a client's situation than I actually do, and recommending actions although I am ignorant of possibly important information
- Acting as if I have more expertise in an area than I actually have, which leads the client to consult with me in matters I really know little about
- Behaving as though the work took longer than it actually did

I confess to having yielded to most of these temptations. Let's be honest: I have yielded to all of them! This is not presented for purposes of public confession, but to emphasize that we consultants have many ways of misusing our power in the name of gaining our client's confidence. I am not proud of my misuses of power, but by looking at them, I have a better understanding of why I did this:

- I wanted even more power with my clients than I already had.

- I wanted them to move their organizations in a specific direction.
- I thought that my manipulation of information served some higher purpose.
- I thought that I knew better . . .
- And I will no doubt think so again.

So ego, vanity, expertise, control, and aspirations to the executive ranks are all reasons why we consultants can choose to abuse the powers given to us.

It is impossible for me to draw the line for others on their use of power; I can only draw it for myself—and as the preceding examples indicate, I do not always draw it very straight.

If we are going to presume to help organizations bring about change, we have a responsibility to think through the ways in which we try to influence those organizations. How far can we push our clients? How much should we impose our values on the organizations we work with? What are the limits to our power in organizations? How do our self-perceived limits match with the clients' perceptions? In the following sections I will focus more closely on four possible abuses of that power by consultants in organizations.

Knowing Best

*D*ealing in organizational issues day after day gradually distorts my perspective on what I really know. Combine that experience with the outside consultant role—the role of knowing different or better, of not being involved, and of having new ideas—and I find myself moving from "knowing a more effective way" to "knowing better than" to "I know best!" (with a hint of "I *am* better than . . ."), which means trouble. My clients' expectations reinforce that part of me

that wants to get it all right,
to believe that I really do know what to do all of the time,
that I really am an exceptional consultant and person
with very special talents
that everybody likes

and I can do no wrong
and am generally quite wonderful . . .
Let's face it . . . I am perfect!
There is no need for me to change anything,
and there is every reason for everyone else to listen to me,
to acknowledge my obviously superior wisdom and insight,
and, of course, love me.

Consulting feeds these godlike fantasies in me and here's how: The clients invite me in to help and I do. Wonderful! The clients tell me so. Also wonderful! The clients' actions imply that my kind of talents are what they need around this place full-time. Okay. The clients think that I would work better in this situation than they do. Not so okay. I think I could handle their jobs better than they do. Decidedly not okay. The reality is that if I were in the middle of the mess they are in (let's assume that it is a mess for a moment), I would be another contributor to the mess along with them. I would be as stuck as they are if I had all the history that they have.

I am able to help clients precisely because I am not part of their organization, but an invited and helpful guest. There are some special privileges that come with being an invited guest:

I get attention.
I get to ask dumb questions.
I get listened to.
I can state what I think might be going on without getting mired
 in all the details.
I get to leave when I am through—or any time before then.
I get to say whatever I want to say.

And that is just a sample of all that comes with being a guest called a "consultant." There is much power in these privileges, a power different from that held by people who live there full-time.

This power comes with my role; I am making a mistake if I think that it comes just because of who I am and the skills I bring. I am obviously not irrelevant, but there is much power here that does not originate with me. Maintaining role power depends on my skills, but the power initially comes with the role. I am not trying to diminish my importance, but to put it in perspective.

Perhaps I can demonstrate the point in another way: Look at the organizations, systems, or work units in which you have been involved for a long time as a member, not as a consultant; these may be Little League, church, Kiwanis, friendships, a support group, or family. Think about how you participate in the issues that come to these organizations. When there are problems, do you behave in the same way you do when you are consulting? Do the other members of the organization treat you the same way that your clients treat you? Are you accorded the same respect? Does your obvious wisdom and insight carry the day? Do they care at all about the fact that you are supposed to be something of an expert in helping organizations work effectively?

My answers are no, no, no, no, and no. I find myself trapped in the problems much as my clients are, unable to pull myself through the mire. In fact it is remarkable how mired down I can become, all the while thinking, "I know how to solve problems like this. Why can't I do it?" My children are not impressed one whit with my credentials when we are trying to solve a family problem. I belong to a professional support group of consultants, called the Woodlands Group. We regularly get mired down in problems very similar to those we help our clients resolve.

Knowing that I do get stuck in much the same way as my clients do is useful (if sobering) to me:

- First and foremost, it is the reality; it helps me keep balance.
- Second, I can tell my clients that I get stuck too. They know that I understand what is happening to them.
- Third, they sense that I am not blaming them for being stuck, that I accept them in their present condition—because it happens to me and I accept me.
- Fourth, it emphasizes the obvious (which needs emphasizing)—that I am human too. This keeps them coming back to talk to me directly about their foibles, rather than hiding in embarrassment because they think I will be disapproving.

Knowing a more effective way, or seeing other alternatives, is often possible just because it is not our predicament but someone else's that we are looking in on. In the bigger picture, we are much more like clients than we are different from them. We are the client too. (For more on this from another perspective see Part Two, "Opening the Organization.")

Manipulation

*W*hen I manipulate, I pursue an end without revealing that end or the means I am using to pursue it. It is below the board, intentionally concealed, and devious. I usually know when I am doing it, and I know there are costs if I am found out. Manipulation undermines trust, the primary glue that holds organizations and client-consultant partnerships together, allowing them to be effective.

Having done some manipulating, and having been tempted to do much more, I know its risks. We consultants have unique access to information in our client organizations. Along with that, we often have the ears of the top members of the organization. If we want time with them, our chances of getting it are better than those of most people who work there. And we have the eyes of the organization on us. That attention puts us in a good position to influence what is going on. Our visibility, our influence, our access—all are made possible by a trust bestowed upon us. Everyone expects (or at least hopes) that we will use what we learn in an aboveboard fashion.

That is always my intention, and frankly, it isn't always easy to honor. Organizations are complex places in which to work. During the life of a project it is not unusual for someone to question the way that I am working and whether I am honoring my commitments. This usually comes out of people's discomfort with the risks involved or the changes taking place, but it can also come through mistakes on my part. There are times when, in trying to help, I get in the way. There are times when I use the trust bestowed on me inappropriately. Pretending that I am the perfect consultant is no more believable than my clients pretending to be perfect managers. I attempt to demonstrate my positive intentions toward the organization and to make my trustworthy behavior evident to the client. This provides balance and protection for those times when my perspective or behavior slips.

The prescriptions against manipulation are simpler to express than to honor:

- Tell people why you are dealing with them. Tell them what you want from them and why.
- Tell them what you will do with what you have learned from them, and tell them before you have learned it.
- Before asking where they stand, be open enough to tell them where you stand. Or tell them that you want to hear their position first, but then you will tell them your own.
- Let people know how you are working with them and others to achieve the end you are reaching for.
- Be honest about your differences with others. State your position and state theirs. Point out the differences.
- Respect positions that are different from your own. State your respect.
- Encourage people who take a position different from your own to seek support for that position, just as you are seeking support.

Pretense

I regularly catch myself in some form of pretense. I am not proud of this, but it is the truth.

- I pretend to understand more about my professional field than I do. I act as if I have heard of a concept or a person I have never heard of.
- I toss out a new piece of jargon, implying that I am completely familiar with it when in fact I don't know anything about it.
- I exaggerate my accomplishments and my satisfaction with my work.
- I pretend to be doing more work than I actually am doing.
- I pretend to be doing less work than I actually am doing.

These examples are not rare; they occur daily. Most of the time I am aware when I am presenting myself in a way that does not fit well with the real me. Most of the time. There are times when I fool myself into believing that what I am saying is true, as I do with a favorite story that I made up years ago. The story is one I tell about myself that has the terrific result of making me look good. Ten years ago, that story bore some resemblance to reality, though even then it was distorted to my advantage. Now, after telling the story so many times and improving it along the way, I couldn't tell you what really happened if I had to! I really don't know how big an exaggeration I have caught myself up in. The story has reached the point where the truth is irrelevant—at least in my mind. This is a danger point.

When truth becomes irrelevant, or less relevant, or changes in service to what I want to accomplish, I am in danger of losing my "self." Better put, I am in danger of losing my true self. I know that I am a person who goes through life over-simplifying, exaggerating, and (yes, even) lying in big and small ways to get what I think I want. (Fortunately, I feel compelled to remind you, these are not my only qualities. I am also capable of great honesty with myself and others, but that is not what we are talking about right now.)

Frankly, my smaller transgressions do not trouble me—as long as I know what I am doing. As long as there is a small, but clear, voice inside me saying, "What you just said alters the truth and you know it; you are just trying to impress them." Or the voice may say, "Why do you have to act that way? You know that doesn't fit with how you feel. Who are you trying to fool?" These important internal messages help keep me on track— or close to the track. I worry when the messages quit coming, when I am so caught up in pretending that I don't stop to check with how it fits the real me inside.

Deception

*D*eception is a weightier word than pretense; it is closer to lying. It took me a while to acknowledge that it fits me. For someone in pursuit of growth and authenticity, it is anathema. Yet the longer I live, the longer I do this work, the more aware I am of the differences between how I present myself and who I am. Over the years the gap between these two positions has narrowed significantly while my discomfort with the gap has increased. Too much of that gap is deception;

I am intentionally presenting myself in ways that I know are not authentic. And I have all the "right" reasons for doing this: "They aren't ready to hear this right now." "He wouldn't like what I have to say." "She will feel badly if I tell her the truth." I suspect you know the litany.

I do not see my struggle as unusual. It is a human struggle, not just a consultant's struggle. Given that our most significant growth is toward becoming our potential selves, reducing our deceptive behavior is our day-to-day, minute-to-minute opportunity to grow. Let's look at some of the opportunities in consulting:

> *You are working with a long-term client you know very well. You are uncomfortable with the amount of time it takes the two of you to plan each step in the project. You believe that your client spends too much time thinking through the details of the project, preventing both of you from thinking about the bigger picture. You also doubt that your client is presently capable of thinking in those larger terms. You have not said anything about this and have acted as if the focus on details is all right with you. In other words, you have supported the client's belief that what you are doing together is important when in fact you believe the opposite. The work has become painful to do and you know it is because of the issues that you have not confronted. The client only knows that you are uneasy and unhappy in the work, but does not know why.*

> *You are talking with a potential client. After about an hour, you are quite clear that working with this person or organization would be uncomfortable. In fact, you are sure that you do not want to work with him. He asks if you would be interested in working for him. You respond affirmatively, even enthusiastically, because you don't want him to think that you are uncomfortable with him and because there is a part of you that cannot say no to new work. At this moment, you know that you would rather not work here, but you do not give him any indication of this. You don't*

want him to feel rejected or to think that you are judging him negatively. You want him to continue to see you as a nice person.

A friend, whom you have known over the years through professional associations, calls. She explains a situation that exists at her company and asks you if you would be interested in consulting to the company. You ask for more information about the project, suspecting that it does not fit well with your interests. In the process of telling you more, your friend tells you how she respects your abilities and sees you as the perfect fit for this project. At the same time, you are more sure than you were before that this is not a good fit for you; you could do it well enough, but it does not fit with your current interests or directions. You don't tell your friend any of your concerns because you do not want to say no to a person who obviously thinks so highly of you. Besides, she knows other friends of yours and you want her to continue to say nice things to them about you. You agree to do the work.

These three examples come from my work and I am uncomfortable with the way I handled each of them. My small deceptions build from fears, anxieties, and insecurities I have spent years cultivating. Consulting gives me the opportunity to reinforce those old concerns—or to challenge them.

When I put aside all of the rationalizations of the moment, I recognize that the concerns I have are not generated by the client, but come from within me. I am so adept at disguising my real self that the client usually is not even aware of what I am struggling with. Hours of discussion with friends and consultants have convinced me that I am the source of my own problems:

- I choose to deceive others without involving them in that choice.
- I decide that it would be better if they do not know.
- I decide that they cannot handle it.

- I decide that they are better off in their assumption that I am being honest with them.
- I decide that I know better and that deception is better.

Look at what these decisions say concerning my assumptions concerning the other, apparently unknowing and unsuspecting, person:

- He is not strong enough to handle the truth.
- She wouldn't know how to act.
- His opinions, judgment, and feelings are not as important as mine.
- She would rather know the pretending me than the real me.

I see my concerns about deception as a natural part of my struggle to be authentic in my life and my work. I am laying out my deceptive ways in the belief that exploring them leads to understanding them, and to altering them. Having gone public about who I am and what I do is part of being more authentic—even when the *who* and the *what* are not my best sides. Stan Herman used to call this "busting your own games." Tell people the game you are playing and how you play it. Others will then help you quit playing because they know it's a game. The likelihood of your being able to continue to play your game in the old ways is decreased.

We have talked a lot about fooling others. Now, what about fooling yourself? First of all, it is hard to tell when you are doing it. By definition, you have fooled yourself so you think that what you are saying, doing, feeling, believing is what you really want to say, do, feel, believe. There are at least three sources of guidance available to us at this point: ourselves, others, and time:

- Moving ourselves to a more meditative perspective on the issue of the moment can help us become clear on what we really want versus what we say we want. Time away from the situation that surrounds the issue can help us with that needed perspective. Sometimes just sleeping on it will do the trick. Letting go of our investment in the moment that surrounds the issue and looking at what is important in our work and lives can give us the clarity we need. We can know that we are not fooling ourselves.

- Other people, trusted other people, can provide us with guidance on when we are fooling ourselves. Sometimes, bless them, they just say it flat out: "I think you are fooling yourself." Usually their clues are more subtle, as in, "Are you sure this is what you want?" Or "How does that fit with what you were saying last week when . . . ?" Or "You just don't seem real comfortable with what we are doing." We can ask other people how they are reading us, making it easier for them to compare what we say we want and seem to want.

- We can look back over the years and see ourselves behaving in ways that look ridiculous today. This has something to do with learning. With a few years' perspective, we can often see how we were fooling ourselves in earlier work or relationships or aspirations. Unfortunately, this perspective comes too late to affect the concerns of the moment. But it does point out that we have grown and learned over the years, and that this will probably continue to happen. This suggests that we might pay more attention to today, attempting to understand our present self-deceptions and act on them while we can still do something about them.

PART

Four

MONEY & THE MARKETPLACE

*W*e all must deal with one critical consideration as consultants: We must take care to ensure our survival, with cash flow and clients. In this regard we consultants are no different from everyone else trying to make a buck running a business. My talks with auto mechanics and artists, hair stylists and hardware store owners, find that our business concerns parallel theirs.

In Part Four, I will try to bring unique perspectives to making money in the marketplace. There are dozens of books that can give you the "how to" guidance you may be seeking.

$\overline{13}$ *Making Your Way in the Marketplace*

$\overline{14}$ *Making Money*

$\overline{15}$ *Making the Leap to Consulting*

Though not devoid of "how to," this section is more about "why to."

I should warn you that money and the marketplace are not my primary reasons for being in this business. I see them as important and necessary for survival, because they make possible what is truly important, but I'm inclined to give them as little time as I can.

About four years before I became an external consultant, I started considering it as a possibility. As a part of my consideration, I interviewed a dozen consultants. I asked each of them the same questions and wrote down their answers. This exercise served the combined purposes of educating me, allowing me to talk to people I respected, and delaying my whether-to-be-a-consultant decision. One of the people I talked with was Marvin Weisbord, who said, "What makes a consultant successful is — clients."

The other interviews supported Marvin. There was wide recognition that the primary determinants of success in the marketplace are not based on

who you are or
what you know or
how you are motivated or
how helpful you are or
what you wear or
what your brochure looks like
   or
what kind of car you drive.

Success is based on whether people pay you.

Lots of clients means success; no clients means failure. Certainly there is more to success and failure than this, but at the most basic level, at the first plateau, this is it: clients. I had to put this uncomfortable reality up against some of the more romantic fantasies I had been creating.

The good news, and the bad news, in this message is that it is not personal. Whether I make it is not based on what kind of person I am. It is nice to be able to remind myself of that in tough times, and it is hard to remember when business is thriving.

13

Making Your Way in the Marketplace

Avoiding Selling

Agoraphobia

The dictionary defines *agoraphobia* as "a morbid fear of open or public places . . . fear of the marketplace." Many of us fear being in that open and public place as consultants. To enter the marketplace as a buyer presents no problem; but when we are vendors, and what we are vending is our talent, then it's another

179

matter. We look around at other vendors selling used cars, aluminum siding, carpet cleaning, roach control, or the use of their bodies, and we wonder whether we belong in consulting.

If there were not some fear about this, the world would be waist deep (instead of knee deep) in consultants. The fact that we consultants must ply our trade in the marketplace keeps many people out of this work. That is how I interpret such remarks as: "I really like the work, but I can't imagine knocking on doors." Or "Selling myself to people I don't know is really repugnant to me." Or "If it weren't for the marketing . . ." Or "How could I face a potential client knowing that hardly anyone else is using me and that I need the money!" So the up side of the fear is that it sorts us out. You have to be willing to deal with the marketplace if you are to enter this business on your own.

What I hear from people who have not tried consulting sounds quite different from the reality that my associates and I have known. Marketing and selling your consulting services can be a much richer experience than standing on the curb throwing kisses to passersby. (Well, I think so.) The marketplace is not an easy place for the faint-hearted, but great rewards are possible in facing its challenges.

Sales-Marketing Distinctions

I talk much more about marketing than about sales. That is not just because I think marketing is a nicer word; it's because I try to avoid sales altogether! Instead I spend time helping people understand who I am and what I do. As a result, I seldom ask people I do not already know to consider hiring me. I try to create a world in which my knowledge of the marketplace and its knowledge of me brings appropriate clients to me, asking for my services and eliminating the need for me to knock on their doors offering my services.

For those of you who are doubting my business savvy (or sanity), I'm here to tell you that it works for me. It has worked for me right from the beginning. In twelve years I've made only two significant sales/marketing efforts: once when I went out on my own in Chicago, and again after moving to Seattle. (The Seattle approach is described in "Waiting as a Marketing Tool" later in this chapter. Most advice givers say that you must spend a third to a half of your time in sales. Maybe. But that does not fit with my experience.

I know something of what sales is like, having attempted to sell my services to clients, usually after they've said they want the work done and I know I'm a strong contender. But I don't think my sales techniques have been very effective. When I begin to sell my services to a client, I get uneasy. I feel presumptuous: How do *I* know that they need me?

On the other hand, I am quite comfortable helping a potential client look at his or her needs and explaining what I have done that may fit. I want clients to choose to call me because they need my resources, not because I need theirs. (I hope this distinction is working. It significantly affects how I present myself in the marketplace.)

Business Begets Business

New business comes from two sources: people who know me and my work, and people who have never met me or heard about my work. Those who know me are my primary source of business, and over time this group has expanded rapidly. Business begets business; clients beget clients. Just having made it past the first few years will multiply the potential client base manyfold. For example, I have three clients right now with whom I first worked when they were in other companies. When they moved, they brought me along; in one case, I'm still working with the client's former company.

When I began consulting, my first two clients were people who had previously paid me a salary as an employee. They, and others I had worked with in the past, were essential to my getting started. My new little company grew from old business that I had done, much of it before I was planning to become a consultant. Old business continues to be my primary source of new business. That's one more reason to do an especially good job with today's clients.

I've tried to figure out why people who have never met me decide to call. My best guess is that they've heard of me through someone who has been part of something I have done. I've discovered that usually they've heard of me from at least two sources they respect. I seldom get a call from someone who has heard of me but hasn't checked me out with at least one person who has had direct experience with me. If the pattern I see is real, I can reinforce it, making it more likely that it will recur. The pattern suggests that if I put myself in front of more people at meetings, conferences, and workshops, they will call— or associates of theirs will call. At one level this is not very profound: if more people see me, more people call me.

At another level, this profoundly affects my marketing effort. It says that I can concentrate on doing good work and more work will follow. The good work does not even have to be paid work. I can volunteer to work with groups of potential clients on civic or professional matters. I can stay in contact with people I have worked with in the past, making it more likely that they will remember me and pass my name along. And I don't have to ask anyone for work because the pattern says it will come.

Yesterday I met with a potential new client who called on the recommendation of a woman who works for him. About five years ago, his employee attended a workshop I led for a local professional society as a free professional service. Five years later she recommended me to her new department vice-president. The VP and I had not met until yesterday, and today I have a small project to complete for him.

Waiting as a Marketing Tool

My best marketing is supported by work I've already done for someone else. My challenge is finding ways that will allow potential clients to know that I exist and am available to do similar good work for them. Given my inclinations, I will choose ways that do not intrude on these clients-to-be. I won't be out knocking on doors; I will be sitting in my office waiting. So I needed to learn to wait. I have found it a difficult skill to master, but over the years I've learned that the business world will serve up something I'm interested in doing if I'm patient enough. So far, I haven't been disappointed.

How long is the wait between my initial meeting with a potential client and the call saying that they want to sign me up to help them? *Long!* Far longer than I imagined when I first went into this business. Like most new consultants, I was surprised to find out that a willingness to work with me is not immediately followed by the actual work. Often four, six, ten, fourteen months pass before something that looks like real work begins to happen. So I wait.

While I'm waiting for this new client, I do other things. I go to lunch with friends. I keep in touch with old clients. I mow the lawn. I do work for other clients. I read. In my best frame of mind, I look at the time I have as a gift. And I wait, patiently. The patient part is important because its opposite produces anxiety in me and in the potential clients. I don't need the anxiety because it ruins the time I have to myself to do other things. The potential client doesn't need to see me anxious because no one likes to hire consultants who are anxious.

Presenting Yourself in Person

*T*he primary ways you will present yourself to potential clients will be in person or on paper. I suppose that you could fax your picture and résumé to them, or send a videotape, or contact them through your modem, but most of your first contacts will be in person or on paper.

Before getting involved in the details of presenting the real and paper you, some perspective is important: Before you can market something, you must have something to market. When I apply that notion to myself as a consultant, it tells me that I ought to figure out who I am before I go out and try to sell some of me. My first thoughts are not about how I package myself, but about what my "self" is. If I make my "self" the priority, marketing will fall into perspective. (Return to "The Self" in Chapter One to think more about this.)

Small Matters

How do you present yourself authentically, from your perspective, and effectively, from the client's perspective? I'll tell you about the embarrassingly small ways I wrestle with this question. It involves such considerations as:

- Do I wear the blue suit or the gray suit?
- Should I use transparencies or a flip chart?
- What car will I drive?
- Is it more effective to stand or to sit when recapping my report?
- Can I get by another week without a hair appointment?
- Should I own a "power tie"? (That was hard even to list!)
- What will they be wearing to the meeting?
- What about cologne?

I see those questions gathered in one list and feel slightly ridiculous. I mean, do I *really* spend time on such small matters? With all that is important to do in life, do I give time to these nits? Honestly? Yes. I tend to these small matters because I care about how I am seen. I want to make it easier for my clients to work with me. I don't want to make them leap unnecessary hurdles. I want to present myself in ways that are consistent with who I am and ways that are useful to the client. I open myself to alternative ways of doing all this, just as I ask clients to open themselves to alternatives.

What I do and what I clothe myself and surround myself with are different matters. I can adjust my behavior to the moment, but I cannot carry business cards in four designs, drive three cars, or have my office redecorated for each visitor. I must decide on a business card design, an automobile, and an office decor. And all of these decisions stay with me for a while. They deserve additional attention, as does everything that is part of my work and is put before clients. At the minimum, I try to stay out of my own way. At the maximum, I want to present myself in ways that help convey who I am and what I stand for. Here are some examples:

- When first meeting a client in his or her organization, I pay attention to how people there interact and how they dress. I search myself for similar behaviors and search my wardrobe for similar clothes. When I find those behaviors in myself and use them, I am saying to them, "I understand you people; I respect what you do."

- When I am leading an off-site meeting that depends on informality for its success, I make sure that people know this in time to dress appropriately. I do the same and behave in ways that fit with the casual clothes we are all wearing. The intended message to a management team is, "Let's loosen up our thinking and our relationships. Let's work together in some new ways during this meeting."
- Before picking a client up for lunch, I clean the car. My intent is to communicate, "You are important to me; I looked forward to meeting you and prepared for it."
- If there is time before a meeting, I will arrange the room to suit the meeting's purposes. I attend to seating, comfort, writing materials, privacy—whatever is needed to support the meeting's success. Again, the message is that the client and the meeting are important.
- When I send a client a handwritten note rather than a typed letter, I am trying to tell the client that this is a personal message and I cared enough to write it rather than type it.
- When I invite a client to my office (which is attached to my home), I am saying, "I want you to know more about who I am and what I do with my life—and there is much more to it than work."

The point of each of these examples is the message. I'm not sure how well I deliver the message, but I am very conscious of my intent to have consistency between the work I am doing and who I am.

There is room for variety in consistency. I can be myself in many ways, all consistent with what is most important to me. I don't always have to use the same approach, wear the same clothes, or use the same phrases and thoughts. I can adapt, just as I ask clients to adapt. The better I know who I am and what I want to accomplish, the more easily I can consider alternative approaches that will get me there.

Yes, I also can see room for manipulation and deviousness in this reasoning. I have to be careful not to present myself in ways that do not fit with who I am. If I pretend to be someone else, I end up being all appearance and little honest substance. Experience tells me that when I do pretend, clients figure that out sooner or later.

All of these details have to do with intentionally living life and doing work at the "micro" level. The accomplishment of work's larger tasks includes many micro-decisions and micro-actions. I see them as fine sanding and polishing of the work I am crafting. They are signs of respect for all the components of work. Certainly, they can be overdone, but that does not mean they should be forgotten.

Speaking as Marketing

By "speaking" I mean all those occasions when you put yourself and your ideas before others; for example, in speeches, conference presentations, training sessions, or workshops. I see two important marketing opportunities in speaking: the promotion of the event and the event itself.

- If you are asked to speak to the local chapter of a professional society, you may end up talking to an audience of 50 people. But how many others read about you and your session in the society newsletter? 100? 200? 600?
- The last time I spoke at a national conference, about 300 people attended the session. The brochure describing the conference sessions went out to over 40,000 people. My name and session were not particularly prominent in that mailing, but they were there, and who knows how many people saw them.
- A couple of years ago, I was to keynote a conference in Detroit. The brochure went out to thousands of people. Too few people signed up and the conference was not held. Since then at least three people have mentioned to me that they saw I was speaking in Detroit, and one of them talked with me about doing work for her company. I got the promotion without the presentation.

Attend to the way your name and topic are promoted ahead of time because most of the people who read about you will not be there to hear you. Some of them might like to call you someday to talk with you about how your abilities might fit with their needs. Help them understand who you are by seeing that what is written about you describes you.

This is not a chapter about how to make speeches; go elsewhere for guidance on that. But from a marketing perspective, I have found these ideas useful to me:

- Offer participants something new, now. Do not tease them with what you know and will not share with them. Give them something worthwhile; talk to them about content they can do something about. Make this time useful for them.

- Involve them in ways that show you respect what they know. Build on their knowledge by asking them questions, or having them work with each other and report to the group. Show through your design that you believe they are worth listening to.

- Design the session so they are likely to leave with the feelings you want them to have about the session and about you. Be very clear on what you want them to be saying and doing after the session, then design to produce those outcomes.

- Put aside your worries that if you tell them what you know they will have no need to call you. (If all that you have to offer can be covered in a thirty-minute luncheon talk, they don't need you as a consultant.)

- Use examples of work you have done—examples that will help the audience learn as well as examples that indicate your experience with organizations such as theirs.

- It's all right to indicate that there is a lot more to a topic than you can cover today. It is not all right to say that you do not have enough time to do anything meaningful with them today, and that they really need to spend much more time with you to understand your topic.

- Give them a handout that covers the main points of the session and elaborates on a few of those points. Include your name, address, and telephone number.

- If you want participants' names and addresses, offer to send more materials on your subject to people who leave a business card with you. This yields a stack of cards from people who have listened to you and are motivated enough to walk to the front of the room to give you a card. And in the process, you will end up talking to a few of them. From a marketing perspective, this is real progress!
- Follow up promptly with the mailing you promised. Include a short note to each person, along with your card.

Speaking is a growth opportunity. One of the main advantages of leading a session with a group of people is that you are required to figure out what is important to you and how you can communicate it best. The developmental opportunity for you is in the reflection and planning period that precedes the speech. You have to decide what you want to talk about and how you will do it in a way that at the absolute minimum is not embarrassing, and at the maximum is impressive. One of the best ways to push myself to new learning is to commit to speaking about something I do not know enough about—yet. This commitment combines the avoidance motive (I don't want to make a fool of myself in front of a group of people) and the attraction motive (I gain the opportunity to learn something new and talk with people about it).

I am suggesting that you put yourself at risk today by committing to lead a group of people through a topic about which you know something, but not enough. Of course, don't commit to speaking about something that doesn't promise to be of interest to you, and be sure that you have plenty of time to do the research, the reading, or whatever you need to get up to speed. This caution aside, see this as the opportunity that it is and grow from getting ready for it. I can think of a half-dozen sessions I've led in the last three years that gave me a chance to grow. And I can think of two opportunities coming up, both on topics I don't know nearly enough about to do well right now. It makes me a little nervous just thinking about them. And I am looking forward to the work I will be doing to get ready.

Presenting Yourself on Paper

*T*hink of paper as a conveyor of you to your potential clients. You can shape it, color it, cut it, mark it in any way you wish. Whatever you do with it will be carried to the potential client by the paper. What do you want this person to understand? How do you want to shape, color, fold, and mark the paper to help him or her understand you? Fortunately millions of people before you have answered these same questions. Along the way, they have established some "paper etiquette." That etiquette guides you to some common shapes and colors of paper clients are used to receiving. These papers, organized by size, are as follows:

Business card
Note card
Stationery
Résumé
Brochure
Article
Book

What these papers have in common is that they are all preprinted, usually in quantity, and stacked up to wait for appropriate usage. I will help you think about what you do with these paper conveyors by talking about what I do.

Business Cards, Note Cards, and Stationery

These three interrelated pieces of printed paper are the most flexible and widely used in my work. They share a common design and get redesigned every time I run out of stationery, which is about once every four years. It is hard to design pieces of paper that will represent me well for four years. I'm interested in a style that conveys me now, but I know I'm changing because I look back on my first two designs, both of which I loved at the time, and wonder why I ever chose them.

What will clients think of the card, note, or letter I am sending? What message will be conveyed by its color or design? Will people's reactions be aligned with my intent? I mean, if I intend my card to express the subtle part of me and people receiving it say, "*Wild!!!*" then maybe I missed it. If my stationery requires a battery to keep its neon border lit, then maybe subtle is not its message. My current business card is so subtle that people claim they can only read it in a strong light. Now that certainly has something to do with what I was trying to convey at the time I designed the card. If our clients do not understand what we are trying to convey, we cannot blame them; we are the designers of the paper they are looking at. I'd suggest you hire a professional designer to help you with creative design alternatives.

Résumé and Brochure

There comes a time in every potential business relationship when the client asks for a copy of my brochure. My reaction is always embarrassment: I don't have one and I have never had one. My embarrassment comes out of feeling that I should have one. I really should, you know. I am a consultant and how can I be one without a brochure?

What I do have is three pages about me. First, I have a one-page vita that recounts in exaggerated form some of my accomplishments. I hand this out most often. And occasionally, when a client wants specifics, I provide a two-page résumé listing six recent clients, the work I did for them, and their telephone numbers. All of this information is nestled in my computer, and whenever anyone wants a copy, I print one out on my letterhead stationery. No, it doesn't look like it came from a design studio, but it works. It conveys basic information about me. It also creates a rather homemade impression; I have mixed feelings about this, but I keep on doing it.

Here are the reasons I use to support this homemade approach:

- I can't think of one independent consultant who claims to have gotten a major piece of work because of his or her beautiful brochure.
- I seldom hear stories of independent consultants who have even been called because they had a nice brochure.

- I often hear stories from consultants who designed and printed the brochures they keep carefully stacked in their closets.

- I can keep my three pages up to date. I can modify any one of them to fit the client who asked for the information. A printed brochure would be out of date before it came off the press. I make my homemade product more attractive by using a laser printer.

- I only hand out printed information about twenty times a year. How many brochures would I have to hand out in order to make a large printing economical? One thousand? That's a fifty-year supply! I would probably want to change the contents a bit over the first twenty years or so.

- To write a brochure, I would need to lock in more tightly on what it is I do and want to do. I could do that, but I appreciate the flexibility that comes with a more blurred focus on the future.

- If I were looking for more business, if I had products to market, if I were running a consulting firm, if I liked writing brochure copy—if any of these reasons existed for me, I would design and print a brochure. Those are all good reasons and I may find myself preparing a brochure someday. Today, I would rather write a book—which from one perspective is a very elaborate brochure.

Looking back on all those reasons not to have a brochure, I sound downright defensive about it. Perhaps. I think my real motive is to show a consultant how to save time and money that often has little payoff.

Writing

*W*riting articles and books serves many of the same purposes as speaking opportunities. Most important, they provide you with the occasion to think, alone, about something that is important to you. And if you are to get those thoughts published, they must be put in sentences, strung together in paragraphs and pages in ways that make sense to readers. Publishing offers the further advantage of imposed deadlines that cause you to do what you want to do on schedule, rather than when you might eventually feel like it.

There is an aspect of personal growth and exploration in writing that does not require an audience (beyond you) to bring satisfaction. This has to do with the private conversation you create with yourself through the keyboard and the screen (or paper — though it is hard for me to imagine writing anything of length without a computer). The satisfaction that comes from such writing is similar to the experience of people who keep personal journals. They know they are never going to publish their writings, and yet they give time each day to recording their thoughts. In addition to the growth aspects of exploring your own thoughts, there are meditative aspects as well. Writing removes you at least physically and probably mentally from your day-to-day reality. Your mind moves to a higher plane of thought — though not always easily. The discipline of writing regularly allows you to build a special place in your mind for exercising your thought and recording it "outside," on a disk or a page.

Because this section is about marketing, we will put aside personal journals to concentrate on writing in ways that are appealing to potential clients. Again, I think the best way to write well for potential clients is to write about something that is important to you. Write about work you have done and work you want to do. Motivation is essential to any writing, whether it is an article or a book, so do not waste your time writing about something that you are not interested in. The worst thing that can happen is that your writing will get published and you will become widely known for something that is not part of what you want to do for a living.

So You Think You Want to Write an Article

Most of the advice you need for writing for a specific publication can be obtained from its editor and from reading the publication yourself. Notice what kind of articles it favors, how long they are, what style they use, what content is apparently attractive. Here is the marketing advice that you won't get from the editor:

- Most of the potential client-readers of your article will never see it in a publication. They will see it because you give it to them. Oh sure, there are thousands of other readers who will see your article when it comes out, but how many of them are really potential clients *for you?* Not many, without some concerted effort on your part after the article is published.

- The fact that you are published is more important than where you are published, with the notable exception of a handful of business magazines. When you give an article to a client that is "in print," that is what they notice most of all. You get points because someone else thought your writing was good enough to print. I'm not saying that it makes no difference where you are published; people do notice. But what they notice most of all is that you are published.

- Published materials have a legitimacy that attracts readers to them. The same article straight out of your word processor will get less attention.

- Before you write an article, decide how you will use it from a marketing standpoint. That projected usage will affect how you write the article.

- As most editors will tell you, there is a large chance that your article will not be accepted for publication. Expect that they are right and hope they are wrong. You have many possible uses for your unpublished writing. Success does not depend on someone else's publishing calendar.

- You can use an as-yet-unpublished article as

  A handout accompanying a speech
  An enclosure in a letter to a potential client
  A handout in a training session
  A "gift" in a meeting with a client
  A starting point for a series of articles
  An assignment in a consulting project
  A sample of what a book on the subject might be about

  So the alternative uses of your writing are many and are not limited to being included in the pages of one journal.

- Readers of magazines are often interested in "how to" articles. They want to be able to visualize you doing something that they could also do. The advice I most often get from editors about what I write is to make it less conceptual and more pragmatic. It's good advice.

So You Think You Want to Write a Book

Let me be the first to encourage you! If you were to say that you think you want to have your book published, that is a different matter I will discuss later. As I said earlier, the distinction between writing and publishing is important to me.

What I am writing—and what you are reading—is intended to be a published book. Since you are reading these lines, my intentions were realized. But the larger point is that there are many ways I could use these pages besides making a book out of them:

- Perhaps they will become articles in various journals.
- They might be a series of columns in a professional publication.
- Perhaps this is just an electronic journal, a kind of diary.
- Maybe it is a long collection of "white papers" that I can hand out to clients and associates.
- Perhaps it is two books.

I don't know. What I do know is that all of those alternatives are okay. I didn't have to publish this as a book for this writing to be worthwhile. In fact, for this to be worthwhile I didn't have to do anything beyond sitting here and turning out ten pages a day. Just taking time to think and talk with myself is valuable in itself.

When I wrote *The Quest for Staff Leadership*, I wrote 500 pages before I decided to stop and make a book out of that collection of writing. I felt then as I do now: If my computer had blown up at the end of that 500th page, if every disk had melted and I were left with no record of my days of hard work, it would have been worth it. I learned so much about my thoughts and myself during the writing. Having the record of that learning destroyed would not have destroyed the learning. None of the rewards that have come after completing that 500th page have compared to what I gained from thinking through all those pages. So for me the compelling reason to write a book was the personal growth I gained working with myself. It was so rewarding that my primary motivation for writing this second book is to re-create those rewards for myself; I missed them while I was not writing.

Writing a book comes as close as I ever have to giving birth; I think it is because a book is conceived, nurtured, grown, and carried inside for months before it is laboriously born. If you want to father and mother a child that is very much your own, then give birth to a book. Surround yourself with people who want to help you through the birthing process. Find a caring, nurturing editor. Call on friends who have been through the process themselves. It helps if people shower you with praise when the book is delivered. After my last book arrived, Sheila, my wife, got me a robe and slippers to comfort me through my postpartum depression.

So . . . write a book without worrying about whether it will be published. Write it because it's good for you to do so. Don't worry about what other people will think because other people may never see it. Allow yourself to write without all the worries that come with publishing.

That done, let's talk about publishing for a few minutes. If you do wish to write for a larger audience than your immediate associates, clients, friends, and family, you will become involved in publishing—a world of jargon, contracts, systems, and people you probably have never dealt with before. I have just a few ideas to put beside those that you can get from any acquisitions editor or author:

- First of all, do talk to at least a handful of experienced people about publishing. Open your eyes to that world; you will learn a lot.
- Do not be surprised when none of the publishers seem to want to talk about your book; instead, they will want to talk about the market for the book and how to reach it. So anticipate those questions and think about your answers; they will affect what you write and who is attracted to it.
- If you are determined to have your book published, start writing after you have a contract. Finishing the first

draft of a book and then shopping around for a publisher almost guarantees that you will have to rewrite your book. Publishers have their ideas, too, and they may want you to use many of them in reaching the market.

- Write a book proposal and try it on a number of publishers. What is a book proposal? A written presentation of your intended book—its concept, market, competition, and author. The emphasis is on the market for the book, how large it is, and how it can be reached. Publishers are often surprisingly uninterested in the wonderful ideas you write about. They are very interested in selling books.

- The publishing world is not nearly as creative as I imagined it to be (present publisher excepted, of course). I have found it quite conservative. Conversations with writers and editors show that many of them feel the same way.

- Don't get your book published to make big money. First of all, there just isn't big money in most books that are published. I received one to two dollars from your purchase of this book. (Thank you.) If you want to get rich, the chances are that this is not the way to do it. But . . .

- If you speak two or three times about your book, your fees will probably exceed your book royalties for the year.

Getting a book published can provide a distinctive place for you among all those who consult in your field. It allows people to see you and deal with you as an author as well as a consultant. It may generate speaking opportunities that would not come your way if you had not been published. And because speaking gives people direct experience with you, and because direct experience is the best source of new business, you can see how a book can help broaden your client base.

Writing as a Marketing Tool

This is for those of you who want to combine the developmental opportunities of writing with expanding your visibility in the marketplace: One year after moving to the Pacific Northwest, I decided to learn something about the Seattle business community. At the time, I was doing almost all of my work in other parts of the country. I put together a systematic plan that was very successful in helping me learn more about the local marketplace. It worked well and others have used it successfully, so I will talk about it here. There are three necessary ingredients: a short stack of articles that you have written, a process, and patience. I can provide the process; you must provide the rest.

1. Through library research and a few inquiries, I identified sixty organizations that looked large enough to support my kind of work, no matter who might be doing it. I sorted the sixty companies into three "waves" of twenty companies each. My intent was to work through the twenty companies in one wave before moving on to the next. (As it turned out, I only completed one wave, but don't let that deter you from doing more.) Each wave included a good mix of corporations in terms of the products and services they offered. I thought that would allow me to learn more and make the process more interesting for me.

2. I carefully determined which people I wanted to contact in each of the first twenty companies. I decided to get to know these companies through their human resources managers, because that fit with my own background and the articles I had written. I needed an accurate name, address, and telephone number for the top human resources person and I needed to get that information without talking directly to that person, for reasons that will become clear later. One of the best ways of getting this information was to call at lunchtime when the human resources manager was less likely to be there. Whoever answered the phone usually knew what I needed to know.

3. Here is where my articles enter the process: I sorted through articles I had written and found three that I thought would be particularly useful to a human resources director. I made twenty clean copies of each article.

4. The first Friday of the month I sent each of the twenty directors a personal note, handwritten on note cards with my letterhead. The note said, "I am a consultant. . . . I have written a few articles related to human resources functions. . . . I'll be sending the articles over the next few weeks. . . . Hope you find

them useful. . . ." You get the idea. On the first Friday these notes, with a business card, were mailed without an article.

5. On the second Friday the first article (on appraisal systems) went out with this handwritten note attached: "I know many human resources people struggle with appraisal systems. . . . Here are a few of my thoughts. . . ."

6. The third Friday and the same approach: a second article and a personal note.

7. The fourth Friday and the last article and note were sent.

8. And on the fifth Friday the twenty human resources directors received a typed letter (the first typed material I sent) which said: ". . . Hope you liked the articles. . . . I would like to meet you and learn about your company. . . . I'll be in touch." This letter also included my vita and another business card.

9. About two weeks after sending the last mailing (and two months after the start of the process), I started calling the twenty companies.

The results: I met with eighteen of the twenty companies, usually with the person I had been writing to. Three of the companies called me and asked for appointments before I got to them. In seven or eight of the companies my articles had been circulated. In a few cases my appointment was with a group of people who wanted to talk with me. I learned a great deal about eighteen of the larger companies in the Seattle area. I enjoyed the meetings because I focused on learning about them rather than talking about me. I did indicate how my work related to their work, but I did not offer my services or suggest that they use me. If the process had not resulted in any work I would still have enjoyed it; it would still have been most worthwhile.

It was very time consuming to complete the process as I had designed it. It took close to eighty hours to complete the first wave, from identifying twenty companies to meeting with eighteen. I was busy with clients in other parts of the country and had a hard time following through with my commitment to meet with each company that was interested. (An aside: This difficulty did send a good message to them. My schedule told them that I was in demand.)

The effort was thoroughly successful, just based on the knowledge I gained about the local business community. I dropped the plan to complete the second and third waves because the effort was just too large, considering the time I was willing to invest. And the frosting on the cake was that within the next two years, I consulted to six of the twenty companies I had contacted.

You can adapt this process: Use unpublished articles rather than published ones—that worked well for a friend of mine. Send more or fewer articles. Send your vita or brochure earlier. Establish personal contact earlier. There are many variations. Underlying your success will be how well, how genuinely, the process you create represents you. My process worked for me because it fits with the way I like to work with people. You need a process that fits you as well.

14

Making Money

Valuing Your Services

*L*ike most consultants, I have struggled with putting a financial value on my services. It's hard to know what to charge. When I was new to this work, ignorance combined with insecurity to support the fear that nobody would pay me anything! Then there was the real problem of just saying the words out loud to a prospective client: "My f-f-f-fee is s-s-s-six h-h-h-h-hundred d-d-d-d . . . ," all the while maintaining confident eye contact. Even now, with many fee discussions behind me, I am still hesitant when talking fees, especially when raising my fee with old clients.

Years ago I increased my fees by 50 percent with an established client. There were many reasons, including the fact that it was very important work. I had started out at a lower fee than I was charging others, and my fees were much lower than other consultants this client was using. He asked me why he ought to pay half again as much for me tomorrow as he was paying for me today. My carefully thought-out response (get a pencil; you will want to write this down) was, "Damned if I know!" For similar reasons, he agreed to the increase.

Here we will talk money, what it means, and ways of getting it. What you read here will not prepare you to negotiate, to barter, or to deal. It will help you think about how money is, and is not, significant to what you do and who you are. We will explore distinctions between what you need and what you want, and how that relates to what you are worth. We will consider alternatives for getting your money as well as alternatives *to* getting your money.

Knowing What You Need

> *I don't know what I am worth,*
> *I don't know what I can get,*
> *I wonder what I want,*
> *but I am sure of what I need.*

Let's start with the piece that we can figure out: what we need. I suggest working through this process whether you are a new consultant or have been consulting for twenty years. In fact, the process is probably more important for experienced consultants in danger of losing financial perspective.

I think in terms of two levels of need: what I must have to barely get by and what I want to have to live in reasonable comfort. (One of the difficulties with my distinctions is that you must define for yourself what they mean.) To me, the "barely get by" level is one which could work for months at a time but is not sustainable over years. The "reasonable comfort" level is much less than I would like to have, but is a level I could live with indefinitely. Before I became a consultant, one of the first practical things my wife and I did was calculate those two levels of need.

1. Calculating the "barely get by" level: If money was really tight, how little could we get by on without missing any payments that would take away the house, the car, the children, or the telephone? Our calculation in 1977 was that we needed $1,500 a month just to exist. We could go on in this uncomfortable state for months, but probably not for years. It would not be worth it over the long haul.

2. Calculating the "reasonable comfort" level: How much did we need to live comfortably, where we would feel that the move to consulting was worth it from a family, personal, and professional standpoint, and at a level we knew we could continue indefinitely? Our calculation was $3,000 per month, considerably less than we were currently living on.

3. So we needed a minimum of $18,000 a year to exist and twice that, $36,000, to be comfortable enough to continue consulting—assuming that the work agreed with me and us.

4. How many days a year did I want to work? This is a question my wife and I had already been discussing: One hundred days a year would bring the kind of balance in my life and our family that we were looking for.

5. One hundred divided into $18,000 and $36,000 told us that I needed at least $180 per day to subsist and $360 per day to be comfortable.

6. Time to decide. I looked at what other consultants were getting, at what I was comfortable asking, and at our calculations, and decided to charge $400 per day. That meant that four days a month met my subsistence-level needs; that sounded doable. And eight days a month of actual, paid work would mean comfort; that sounded difficult and maybe doable. It meant that if I could meet my paid work goals, I would still have plenty of time for marketing, family, administrative work, and friends. So it was decided!

Those six steps did not happen for us in quite so orderly a fashion, but we did work through all those decisions. And you can too. Your needs are different from ours, but just as compelling. Notably absent from this six-step process is any consideration of what the client is willing to pay or what the going rate is for consultants like you. These six steps don't talk about your contribution or about results in the client organization. All this is important; it is just not what we are discussing right now.

You must meet your needs if you are to survive as a consultant. You have to charge a fee that will meet your needs if you want to survive—whether you think you are worth that fee or not! The whole process is aided by keeping needs low enough to be met easily. The secret is not large fees, but small needs. It helps not to be too acquisitive or greedy.

What You Charge and What You Are Worth

*C*alculating my needs ties to an underlying belief of mine: Whatever I charge, I am not worth it. My work is worth something, but there is no accurate way of determining what that worth is. At least I have not found a way that satisfies me. And it has become surprisingly freeing for me to acknowledge that I don't know what my work is actually worth and neither do my clients. I know how much I want and my clients know how much they want to pay. So I get paid what I want when that fits with what my client wants to pay.

Let's not cloud this point with precise worth. My work is of value, but what I get paid is what I agree to. The expertise I bring to the work, how well I use that expertise, how hard I work, how much my work actually contributes—all of these important factors do not have much to do with what I get paid. The marketplace, my notion of it and the clients', is much more important than any of these more work-related factors.

So we are not talking about what I am worth. We are not talking about what you are worth. We are talking about what you and I can get for working for others. Your ultimate value is not being put on the line in this decision. The way you decide what to charge, and the way other people decide what to pay you, doesn't have anything to do with your expertise, experience, or the contribution you are making in the world. This is not a question of ultimate worth; it is a question of the marketplace, which is not noted for its contemplation of life's meaning. Whether you are a worthwhile person is not even part of this consideration.

I am emphasizing this point in various ways because most of us struggle with putting a financial value on who we are. That is the wrong struggle, and we lose a little bit just by engaging in it. It takes energy to wrestle with the question of our value in the world. If we insist upon struggling, we ought to put our energies into figuring out what we can get in the marketplace for our work. What are clients paying others for work similar to the work you want to do? Ask other consultants. What do you want clients to pay you? Ask yourself.

One friend I learn from, whose expertise I respect highly, has been struggling to establish himself as a consultant for years. I have another friend I don't learn much from though he is a lot of fun to be with. His expertise is limited to a narrow, even shallow, realm (which I would mention except that he might be reading this) and clients hire him to talk about this over and over again. For lots of money. If you are holding up expertise as your standard, this doesn't make sense. I could give other real examples contrasting people's experience levels, or how hard they work, or the impact they have on the bottom line. In every case I can find consulting fees or success that don't make sense, just as corporate salary differentials don't make sense, and rock stars' incomes don't make sense, and teachers' salaries, and sports figures, and nurses, and . . .

Figure out how much you want and tell clients that. "I want $50 a day for this work." Or "I want $5,000 a day to do this work." A couple of things can make this easier: You initiate the conversation; don't wait for the client to ask. Deal with the subject when *you* choose to. Tell your clients how much you want rather than what you charge. For example, I feel a little stronger saying to an old client, "Starting the first of the year, I want $900 a day for my work with you," than I do saying, "My fee goes up January 1st; it will be $900 a day." The "I want . . ." statement is stronger for me because it is true; I *do* want to raise my fee. It is easier for me to say so directly. As I tell clients what I want, it is implied that they can tell me what they want. The second statement is impersonal by comparison and presented as a fact with no room for movement. Of course there are alternatives, but try the "I want . . ." statements on for size.

Ways of Getting Paid

*7*t is not just what we get paid, but how we get paid. This is affected by prevailing practices, the type of work you do, the preferences of your client, and what is comfortable for you. The best way to decide which of the many alternatives to use is to ask other consultants who do your type of work in your area. Talk with a half-dozen of them about how you should be paid and what you should be paid. There are no correct and universal answers. Here is a range of alternatives I've seen used by consultants:

Per diem.   For each day you work you get a day's pay, the amount agreed to ahead of time. It's simple, open ended, and not related to results.

Fixed amount.   You agree with the client to do the work for a certain amount. This is based on your educated guess, but in the end you get the same amount of money whether it takes you more or less time than you thought.

Variable amount.   You quote the client an estimated cost for the project and get the client's support. You keep track of your time on the project and keep the client informed on your accumulated costs in relation to your estimated costs. The two of you adjust as necessary.

Retainer.   The client pays you a given amount per month to have your services available. Clients pay you whether they use you or not. If they want to use you more than a defined amount, they pay you more.

Product.   You sell a tangible product that stays with the client after you have gone. It may be a workbook, a newsletter, a piece of software—something you sell the client on a unit-by-unit basis. It earns money for you apart from the effort you are investing directly in the client.

Percentage. Your pay is determined by the contribution you make to improving the unit you are consulting to. Measurable results are agreed to ahead of time. For example, you get 3 percent of any improvements in scrap reduction over the next two years.

Equity. You are paid with stock or stock options. You buy into the company with and through your work. You and the client agree on how much equity you get for your work or its results.

Barter. You work in exchange for a product the company offers. For example, your client, an electronics firm, manufactures some wonderful computers. They take a retreat with you; you take a computer from them.

Goodwill. Virtue is its own reward. Your help is widely appreciated by the organization. They praise you to the high heavens. Your reward is knowing you have made a significant contribution to this client, if not to humanity.

These various fee forms may be used in combination. Related expenses may or may not be included. I have extensive experience with the per diem and goodwill alternatives and hardly any experience with the others. So I will talk about what I know about and leave it to others to fill you in on the other alternatives.

Being paid a daily rate simplifies the financial side of working with my clients. They know that if I am working for them, the meter is running. It is easy for both of us to keep track. This arrangement has the advantage (to me and I think to the client) of not narrowing our focus to just the immediate project. We can go where the work takes us, based on the needs of the organization. There is room for innovation. I frequently work on projects that are defined quite openly in the beginning. And it is often difficult to sort out my contribution from everything else that is happening. My open-ended work lends itself to this simpler day-to-day approach.

There are many down sides to doing it this way. First of all, per diem pays for activity, not results. Second, I do not share in any financial gains created in the organization through my work. Another down side is that I only make money when I am working. It is easy to calculate what I earn because I only have to multiply my days worked times my daily fee. This is very limiting, given that there are many alternatives for making money where the amount is not precisely related to the time spent working. As a friend puts it, "I am looking for ways to make money while I sleep!" Per diem is not one of those ways. Unless I alter my ways, when I am a very old man I will still be paid according to the time I invest with the client. Not a pleasant thought when combined with old age.

The Consultant's Line of Credit

For those clients who want to use me for short consultations on a regular basis, I have set up a little system that works well for everyone and cuts down on paperwork. First of all, it must be evident to the client and to me that a pattern of short meetings is emerging—whether on the telephone, through a computer network, or in person. When that is clear, I propose something like this (with you as my client):

"We both recognize that you and I have been working together in short meetings, on and off, for two months. Right?"

"It looks like this will continue indefinitely. Right?"

"You want to pay me for this work and you feel awkward about calling me on short notice. Right?"

"I want to be paid for it and the billing process is awkward for me. Right!"

"So I propose that I send you an invoice for two days of work, as yet not done."

"You pay the invoice, knowing that you can call me at any time and ask for my help. If I am available, I will help, and keep track of my time."

"When I have used up the time you have paid me for, I will tell you and ask if I should send you another invoice."

This process has worked well for me with a number of clients. It keeps them thinking about using me and it keeps me involved in their organizations. It puts the money in my hands up front, demonstrating their commitment. It allows me to fill slack time with their work and does not require that I make adjustments with other clients. One of many variations is for me to bill the client after the work is completed. This works fine, but not as well, in my experience, as billing in advance.

Ruminations on Remuneration

*H*ere is a short collection of ideas that have helped me quantify my contributions:

- I discourage you from going in to negotiate fees with a client. I encourage you to figure out what you want and ask for it.
- When you have decided what and how you are going to charge your clients for your services, stick to it. Do not try to adapt your fees to each client who comes along. Charge the same fee for the same service to clients in the same geographic area. Try to hold onto this fee structure for at least one year.
- Instead of negotiating on fees, negotiate on the work to be done. When a client is concerned about your fees being too high (I've only had one case of a client who thought I charged too little), discuss what work needs doing and how much money the client is willing to pay to get it done. In the process, you can usually find ways that meet both parties' financial needs. Perhaps a piece of the work can be left out, or data can be gathered from fewer rather than more people, or a report may include less than you originally intended.
- Rather than lowering your fee, give clients some time. For example, if the project will take five days and you charge $1,000 a day, but they only have $4,000, bill

them for four days at $1,000 per day and give them the fifth day for nothing. This way you get the work, they get their work done, you are seen as generous, they owe you, and you have not reduced your fees.

- A variation on the preceding item is to do all that but not tell them that it took you five days instead of four.

- An important reason to hold to a consistent fee is to be fair to your other clients. How fair are you being to them if you are willing to do similar work for less money across town? Granted, you deal with them separately and each contract is agreed to by each client, so no one is being cheated. But I feel better knowing that I am being consistent in a way that is easily understood by everyone.

- Consistency does not mean that you have only one fee; it means that you are consistent in the fees you have. For example, I charge significantly more to work out of town than I do for work in town. I also charge more for training groups than I do for consulting to individuals. And I charge in yet another way for speeches to conferences or corporations.

- I do not want to work so close to my financial line that I have to worry about every minute I am working for a client and whether I am being paid for it. I want to keep my attention on my work, and I do that partly by reducing worries about money. I charge clients enough per day so that I am comfortable working extra time for them. When I am in doubt about whether or not to charge for time I have worked, I usually do not charge the client. And I encourage you to do the same. Some examples:
  - If an eight-hour day stretches into ten, I am not concerned. I am paid well for the day whether it is eight or ten hours long.
  - If a client calls and we end up spending thirty minutes on the phone talking about upcoming work, fine. Chances are I won't bill the client for that time; it is just part of the contract.
  - Occasionally, with a client for whom I've done a lot of work, I will do a day's work without charge—if it is work I really want to do. No one

has ever asked me to do this, but I have done it voluntarily a few times. I think it demonstrates my commitment to them and the work.

- I try to do a significant amount of community work each year. I don't charge for it, or I charge for it and return the money. This free work is made possible by all of the for-pay work that I do. I can give that time away because my regular clients pay me well.

Slippery Success Indicators

For three years I maintained an elaborate spreadsheet on my computer. Picture it:

In the
left-most
column,
listed
alphabetically,
were my
present,
past, and
potential
clients.

Across the top, columns were headed: Client, Content, Initial Contact, Estimated Work Days, Daily Fee, Contracted Work Days, Days Worked, Date Invoiced, Amount Invoiced. Each month I would update this spreadsheet; my whole work world would be displayed before me. In appropriate columns, totals would automatically total. I could see at a glance how many days I had worked, how many I had contracted for, and how much money I had made. It took some time to use, but it was terrific!

I turned the spreadsheet over to a part-time employee (and full-time family member). I sent him little slips of paper that instructed him what to enter into the spreadsheet. And he sent me back . . . nothing! So I sent more little slips of paper with very clear instructions. Still nothing. The spreadsheet became out of date and useless, and died. I became angry. My employee continued not to see the problem.

Cut to six months later: I am standing at the bathroom sink, looking into a lower-left-hand drawer. I see soap, lots of soap, little bars of soap with hotels' names on them. There must be fifteen little bars of soap. I start thinking about where they came from. I can tell from the number of bars that I have been traveling a lot lately, and I have been working for clients who put me in some very nice hotels where I steal the soap as expected. There's some Neutrogena®, and some black soap in a little plastic box. Not much Ivory® or Camay®. Looks pretty good in the soap drawer today. And my feelings about the amount of work I have, and my bank account, are pretty good too. Hmmm . . . I begin to notice a possible relationship between the amount and type of soap I am collecting and the amount and type of work I am collecting.

Four months later, same scene: I am looking into the bathroom drawer and it is—practically empty! All the good soap has been used up! I am down to a broken bar of Safeguard®. Could it be? I look at my checkbook and, sure enough, it is almost as empty as my soap drawer! I look at my calendar; it looks pretty bare too. I haven't been doing much work over the last month or so. *Aha!!* There *is* a direct relationship between the amount and type of soap in my drawer and the amount and type of work in my calendar!

Needless to say, I have not reactivated my electronic spreadsheet. No, my soap drawer doesn't tell me everything, but it does convey the essential messages. And my suspicion is that its emptiness is a leading indicator (by about two months) of what will be happening in my refrigerator.

Contracting Is Vital; Legal Contracts Are Not

*D*one well, all of our early marketing considerations will yield clients who want to use our unique combination of abilities and are willing to put their resources behind their wants. Now it is time to reach a common understanding with those clients.

There is nothing more important to the consulting process than attending to contracting. As other sections have emphasized, you must attend to it constantly because it is alive and always moving, changing, and adapting to what is happening. The client and consultant need to be mutually clear about what each expects of the other and what each is going to provide the other. Contracting is an exchange of wants and needs going both ways. It starts with first contact and is alive, and being renegotiated, throughout the entire consulting relationship. Either person can open a discussion of this living contract at any time. If my needs as a consultant are different now than they were yesterday, then I will open a discussion. If the wants of a client are going to be different tomorrow, he or she should discuss that with me today.

My contracting differs from a legal contract. My reservation about legalistic contracting concerns what happens to the partnership while the legal document is being created. A legal document, once it is finished, is more dead than alive. Contracts that emphasize form more than substance kill the client-consultant partnership. Contracts that are legalistic have the same effect on our relationships with our clients that prenuptial agreements have on marriage. Even when they are necessary, they are not very romantic, and certainly not what the partnership is all about. I avoid them whenever possible.

I attempt to create a contracting process with my clients that is alive and adaptable, not one that is fixed in ink. I encourage trust between client and consultant. I see anything that smacks of mistrust—as defensive legal contracts can do—as damaging to the partnership I want to establish. I favor written communication that records what we decided so we don't forget our responsibilities. I keep files tracking the work the client and I are doing together, but I balk at anything written that suggests we need to protect ourselves from each other.

I have never required a client to sign a contract with me. I have only been "burned" once in twelve years and then not badly enough to cause me to reconsider my practice of "our word is our bond."

Clients occasionally require some form of contract of me and I am usually willing to sign what they put together. I'm not ornery about it; I just don't encourage the practice by giving it attention. If all that is required of me is a signature, I'll sign. If the legal contract begins to intrude on our work discussions, I get concerned.

At the same time, I must acknowledge that most of the major problems I had when I was a client, and that I have had as a consultant, can be traced back to poor contracting. I hasten to add that the problems would not have been solved by a legalistic document or process. Instead I would criticize my lack of clarity, inattention to detail, failure to keep up with changes, or misunderstanding of the other person's intentions.

I know other consultants who are more structured and contract oriented in their dealings with their clients. If this works well for them, I would not suggest that they stop doing it, only that they reconsider its necessity. Just because it is a barrier for me does not mean that it is a poor fit for everyone. I also know that my contractless approach is possible because I'm a one-person firm taking on projects of limited scope. But whatever the size and nature of your consulting business, watch out for relationships that focus more on the written word than on what is happening between the people involved. (*Peter Block's book,* Flawless Consulting, *provides an excellent description of a contracting process.*)

Now that my biases are clear, how do I integrate my need for a living contract with the need for a written memory of what we are doing together? Following a lengthy discussion or negotiation with a client, I find it useful to outline in a letter the major points we covered and the actions we each plan to take. I see this as confirming our contracting rather than being a contract in the legal sense. I will do whatever I can to make sure that the client and I understand each other; reinforcing our face-to-face work with a letter just makes sense. It gives us a mutual record of what has happened.

In my early years as a consultant, I spent a lot of time talking with clients about what I would do and they would do, and how we would continue or end this contract, and how often we would stop the project to take a look at how it was proceeding, and so on. Some clearer understanding came from that; clients cooperated in my need to do it, and I am sure some problems were avoided. But it took up a lot of time, time that could have been spent on the work at hand. Lately I find it useful to make a few more assumptions about how we are going to work together, to reinforce actions that fit with my assumptions, and to question actions that do not.

To me this is similar to dancing with someone you have never danced with before. You and this new dance partner do not have to go through a long negotiation about when you are going to dance, who is going to lead or follow, or how long you will dance. There is usually an invitation, an acceptance, and a dance. You learn from each other as you go along what each needs to do to allow the dance to work.

Similarly, important contracting happens not just at the start of the client-consultant partnership, but throughout the work. It is much less important to me than it used to be to stop working/dancing in order to talk about how things are going. More often, I try to check regularly on how we are doing as we work.

My current practice is to begin the contracting with more positive assumptions about how the client and I will work together and to put fewer concrete details in the initial contracting process. Then I watch to see how those assumptions are borne out in the work, and I continue contracting as the work calls for it. I see to it that the client and I have a clear understanding of what will happen between now and our work horizon. And I don't spend much time contracting for what is over the horizon. I find clients more drawn to this approach than to my process-laden contracting of a few years back. I also find that we get more work done and our contracting is more relevant because it's more timely.

Clients Want Consultants Too Busy to Work for Them

*W*hen I need work—I mean, when *I need* work—it is very obvious to me. My mental and emotional wheels shift to a higher gear. My ability to say no is bound, gagged, and thrown in a deserted back room of my mind. My head feels compelled to nod yes and affirm everything the client says. In my mind I'm not thinking about the work, but shouting, "Hooray! House payments! Car payments! College tuition payments! Credit card payments! Food!" I am focused on the money.

I am bothered by the disconnection between what I am thinking about and what I am saying to the client. Being "hungry" does not qualify me to do this work. It doesn't disqualify me either; it is simply not relevant to the client's needs. When my external messages are out of synch with my thoughts, I get concerned; I know that I'm pretending to be something that I'm not. And that is the path to dissatisfaction with myself and my work.

While I am going through my gyrations, what is the client doing? To begin with, many clients are suspicious of consultants, an often well-founded suspicion, as I see it. And they get especially suspicious if they think that this consultant, me, needs the money and is acting as if he does not. They want me to be busy on twelve projects similar to theirs in major corporations that they respect. They want years of expertise backing my every move. They want me to be in such demand that it is amazing if I have time for another project. They want me not to need the work or the money. So when they see dollar signs begin to flash in my eyes, that is a turnoff. When they hear me pushing to get the work without ever leaning back to consider it, that is a turnoff. When I don't even have to look at my calendar to see if a date is available, but just agree to anything, and when afterward they see me leaping with joy around the company parking lot (with my entire family, which has been waiting in the car), this does not bring a similar joy to the client's heart!

Okay, I've exaggerated, but you get the point. Somehow I, you, must maintain a perspective that separates our needs from the clients'. We need to meet our needs by meeting theirs, rather than vice versa. And this is especially important early in the contracting process.

15

Making the Leap to Consulting

*T*his chapter is directed to those who are considering consulting and those who are new to external consulting. It is intended to help you decide what you want to do. It deals with some of the problems of flying out of the corporate nest. It considers alternative work structures and appraises the importance of academic preparation. Though none of these considerations is unique to starting out, this period is particularly loaded with such thoughts.

Preparing for the Leap

*B*ecause I spent about fourteen years inside companies before cutting the corporate umbilical cord, many people ask me how I did it and how they can do it. I am certain that I don't know all the answers to those two questions, but here are some answers offered to provoke your thought.

About halfway (seven years) into my corporate career, I began thinking about whether I might want to be a consultant one day. Before that—yes, *before* that—I did some other things that ended up being quite useful to me later. (I am emphasizing this because I unintentionally prepared myself to be an external consultant; you could do it on purpose.) Here is what I did:

- I wrote and published an article a year.
- I co-led three or four public workshops a year.
- I presented papers once or twice a year at conferences.
- I spoke to a few civic organizations.
- I attended at least one public workshop a year, putting myself in contact with consultants and people from other companies.

I did this because it helped me develop, or because I wanted professional recognition. These efforts each took time and didn't make any money. I wasn't planning to be a consultant then, but in retrospect I see how helpful each was to what I now do.

The primary boost in my eventually launching myself as a consultant was the work I did for three Fortune 500 corporations. Much of the time I was an internal consultant, doing work closely related to what I do right now. I loved the work and loved working for large organizations. This positive experience significantly affects how I work with clients now. They can see that I love this work and respect them for what they are trying to do. They know I believe that people can find life's meaning through their work in corporations. They do not see me as someone who hates corporations but is forced to leech off them to make a living. Quite the opposite.

My corporate work also served me well because while I was there, I don't think I ever aspired to rise in the corporate hierarchy. I wanted to do interesting work and I went after it.

At times this hurt me politically; it certainly didn't fit with the behaviors of people on more career-oriented paths. I was able to involve myself in important work without the distraction of wondering whether I would be a vice-president someday. So I acted like an independent consultant even when I was a dependent consultant, preparing for my present role.

In my first professional position, I was assistant to a vice-president and dealt regularly with executives. So as a junior person, I learned not to be intimidated by the top people in the company and that has served me well.

About half of my corporate years were spent in supervisory or managerial positions. I learned what it is like to have a group of people to lead and manage. Along with this came experience in the power and politics of organizations.

Each of these areas—external work, writing, workshops, conferences, love of the work, project rather than career orientation, early executive contact, management experience—serves me well now, and some of them help define my uniqueness with my clients.

I began to get serious about the leap four years before I made it. I interviewed a collection of consultants, asking them how to do it, what it was like. I probably would have gone into consulting then had I not been contacted about a unique job opportunity. My eventual decision to go out on my own was less rational/analytical than it was intuitive. It came as a surprise to me in a conversation with my wife.

She had just returned from a three-week summer trip; we were discussing what had happened in the interim. While talking about work, I heard myself finish a sentence with, ". . . and at the end of the year I think I'll go into consulting." Imagine my surprise! I hadn't even been thinking about consulting, at least not on a conscious level. Her response, "If you want to do that, I will support you," sealed the deal. We started working in that direction from that moment. That was five months before I took the step.

A few weeks later I told my staff and my boss. I recommended to my boss that he promote one of my people to my job and hire me as a consultant for part of the next year. He agreed, partly because there was a net financial saving in the agreement. Then I went to an earlier employer and sought work with that company. It came. Two months before I actually cut myself loose, I had signed up more than half the work and income I needed for the coming year. So I wasn't leaping off into space. Those votes of confidence buoyed me up for the big step and were also useful as I talked with other prospective clients. I had business to point to; somebody wanted to use me, and those first two clients were both previous employers.

All those years in corporate life made it especially important to me to say that my previous employers valued my work. And what better evidence than having them as clients!

I offer that story primarily because it could be of use to you as you consider making a similar leap. It helps to have one foot planted on the ground while the other, poised in midair, searches for solid footing in the marketplace.

Building a client base can start years before your actual move to external consulting. You could set about building your base more intentionally than I did. There are three especially useful parts to that foundation: a list of potential clients, a stack of published articles, and a number of completed presentations.

Clients. Start thinking about the move to consulting and working on it years ahead of your actual move. Keep track of the people you work with who are potential future clients. Especially note their movement to other companies and the positions they hold there. Collect addresses and phone numbers that you might use later; you will need them to track your contacts down. My first seven clients included five people with whom I had worked closely in the previous six years. If I had known that would be the case, I would have prepared better for it.

Like other people trying to make a sale, we will probably start with those who know us and our work best. Insurance salespeople start with relatives; we start with former associates, employers, and internal clients. Three-fourths of my earliest work came from people I used to work with. And, let's face it, if your former associates are not willing to hire you, why should complete strangers be interested? You may have a good answer for that, but it is a consideration.

Articles. Start publishing now. Ten years before I became a consultant I began writing an article a year. It turned out that years later those articles were of wider value to me as a consultant. Some of them served as handouts to potential clients and in training sessions. All of them served to distinguish me a bit from that large crowd of consultants from whom potential clients have to choose. And these articles gave me a little name recognition in a few places. So what I accomplished with my articles was different from my motivation for writing them. You don't have to learn about this belatedly: Start publishing now! I know many external consultants who would like their names on a few articles today, but the review process for most journals makes it close to a year before anything they submit is in print, even if it gets accepted.

Presentations. Many professional organizations are crying out for presenters at their monthly meetings—especially if you are not a consultant. Use the position you have as a corporate insider (who is not trying to sell anything) to your advantage. Talk with professional groups in the area about what you are doing in your company. In the process, people get to know you. Offer to train people in subjects that are of interest to you (and that will eventually be part of your consulting repertoire). Many national conferences are looking for presenters who want to share their companies' experiences.

On Doing Without and Being Alone

*T*he most important differences between being inside and being outside are not skill related. You need the same kinds of skills in both positions. So what is different?

You will probably notice the absence of a regular paycheck,
    and the health benefits,
    and the paid sick leave,
    and the retirement plan.
No one sorts your mail or opens it,
    or makes copies for you,
    or types a letter,
    or answers the phone,
    or buys books for you,
    or gives you an expense account
    or paper clips.

No one trains you,
   or tells you what the policy is,
   or keeps you up to date on where the company is going,
   or passes on gossip.
No one finds work for you,
   or assumes that you are the one who is going to help them,
   or expects you to be around two or three years from now.

There are many resources at your disposal on the inside that just flat disappear when you go outside. The further up the hierarchy you are now, the more you will notice the resource gap when you leave.

I am intentionally not discussing the skills needed for consulting; instead I'm focusing on other factors that affect motivation. Unhooking from your corporate support systems has implications for your motivation, your personal power, and your energy. My concern is helping you understand how you want to use yourself as an external consultant. What do you expect to get out of being an external consultant? Your answers better come from your heart and not from your head. The lack of external support in the form of an organization, a salary, a role, a direction—all of this has to be made up internally. External consultants have to go internal, inside themselves, to find the motivation to survive out in the world—alone.

Choosing to be an independent external consultant means choosing to be alone. Not all of the time, but certainly much more than our counterparts in corporate life, or even those in consulting firms. Getting comfortable with being alone is critical to thriving as a consultant on your own.

I am reminded of divorce: Two people who have spent years together choose to live apart. One of the first things each must learn is how to live alone, how to be responsible for his or her own life without being in a relationship with another person. Leaving the world of large organizations and setting up shop in a spare room is similar to divorce. From the beginning, I noticed how quiet it was . . . how the phone seldom rang . . . that there was no one to have coffee with . . . that I had to decide what to do next . . . that there were no other offices to wander into . . . that I had no associates to chat with. To put it bluntly, no one seemed to care what I did or said! I was not nearly as important as I had been a few days earlier, back in the office!

Years in corporations blinded me to my dependence on their people, systems, structure, and culture. So much of what I did was in relation to, in support of, this organization, and that gave me meaning. I was surprised to discover this dependence; I really thought I was more self-determined than that. (Or maybe I had been determined to become dependent on the corporation.)

There is an old story that seems related: A couple lives right next to the railroad tracks in the city. Every morning at 3:37, every morning for *years*, an express train roars past their bedroom window. This morning at 3:37, there is no train, no roar. When the train does not go by, they both awaken suddenly, frightened out of their sleep, exclaiming, *"What was that!??!!"*

"That" in my case was the absence of the corporation; it did not arrive on schedule at the beginning of my day as it had for fourteen years. And the silence was deafening and frightening.

We are not condemned to isolation. There are alternatives: joining a consulting firm, forming a consortium, building a professional support group. We can find ways to meet some of the needs that were met in the corporation. The complication is that we must also make a living. Spending most of an afternoon chatting around the company had little evident impact on our paychecks. Opportunities to earn more were not necessarily lost. Doing the same thing as an independent—and doing it regularly—can be costly.

When your needs for nurture push aside your pursuit of business, notice. When you are lonely and find yourself seeking out relationships like those you had back at XYZ Corporation, while delaying the contact you need out in the marketplace, watch out. If this becomes a pattern, consider whether you really do want to have your own one-person business. A number of my consultant friends have chosen to join larger firms, to take partners, or to go back into corporate life because of this need to be affiliated with others. Some of these consultants were doing quite well financially but their "people" needs were not being met. Others were not doing as well financially; their need for comrades blocked their motivation to find work.

And what do I do about it? First of all, though I love working with others, I don't need to be with them all the time. My more introverted side is supported by the time alone that this work gives me. Second, I have large telephone bills. I call friends and associates across the country; that takes care of many of my social needs. Some of my friends in the profession have commented that I take good care of them with my regular calls and notes. Actually, I am taking care of myself. Third, I belong to a professional development and support group that meets quarterly. And of course, there are my few especially important local friends; we get together on a regular basis.

As with a divorce, it takes some time to adjust and learn about being alone at work. After the initial exhilaration of starting the business wears off, after having told everyone (three times) about how exciting it is to do this, after designing the letterhead and business card—after all that, you come face to face with . . . yourself. There is no one else there. What are you going to do now? Not having done this before and coming from a long relationship you could count on, you will be uncertain and awkward. And why not? Why should you be so good at this?

This awkwardness and uncertainty is filled with potential and excitement. One of the best reasons to become an independent consultant is to learn about yourself, and that opportunity greets you very quickly—though it may be costumed in ways that alarm you more than encourage you.

Lone Consultant, Associate, Partner?

7 see at least three reasons to associate yourself with others in a firm rather than being on your own:

- Personal inclination—if you like working with others more than being alone.
- Business—if you don't have any and others do; if they are established and you are not. Add to this a discomfort with marketing and selling yourself, and you are leaning in the direction of affiliating yourself with a firm.
- Abilities—if the skills you possess currently are too narrow to stand on their own in the marketplace, or if you can learn skills important to you by being part of a firm.

Most people associate themselves with a firm for one of the last two reasons. Many see it as an interim step to being completely on their own. As a result, consulting firms are busily engaged in training their associates to be the eventual competition. The contracts signed on entering a firm are getting more and more complicated as firms try to protect their business from departing associates. Let that serve as a caution for those of you who plan to use someone else's business as a stepping-stone toward your own.

Some consultants have been successful working together in something less than a firm, a kind of loose affiliation of professionals. They refer business to each other. On a project-by-project basis, they decide on financial arrangements. They support their loose structure because they want to continue to work with each other. The variations on this theme are many, and most of them are outside my experience. It seems to me that an affiliation based on mutual needs and skills would be likely to hold together better than one based primarily on financial considerations. In other words, you cannot pay me to work regularly with someone I do not want to work with.

Subcontracting

*I*f you are new to consulting and do not have much business, someday you may contact other consultants about the possibility of working for them as a subcontractor. If you have been a consultant for a while, someone may contact you about the possibility of doing work for you as a subcontractor. Subcontractors do work that contractors/consultants do not have the time, expertise, or inclination to do. They offer to provide the contractor with the services needed in return for money. The contractor usually bills the work out at a rate higher than the amount he or she is being paid, making money on the difference. What are the primary considerations involved in this arrangement?

First, as a contractor: By using subcontractors you can make money on the difference between what you pay the subcontractor and what the client pays you. In other words, you get paid extra for finding the work and taking responsibility for the whole project. The subcontractor is paying you for finding the work. On a long project, this could be sizable and worth it. A contractor of others' services becomes more like an employer; she or he becomes responsible for the subcontractor.

I seldom contract the services of others. I see this as a burden, so I will search for other reasonable ways of getting the work done. Instead, I ask the consultant to work with me, and I help him or her develop a relationship with the client. The client pays that person directly. I don't need the extra hassle of being the middle man in order to make money.

Let's consider ourselves as potential subcontractors: I know a handful of people who make most of their living working for other consultants. Doing this successfully allows them to avoid the marketing/sales side of consulting work while learning and contributing. Of course, they are limited in the work they do to what the contractor finds.

Many subcontractors struggle with the fact that they are getting billed out at a rate that is higher than the amount they are being paid. They wonder why they should have to accept this lower rate for work the client is obviously willing to pay more for. In this, their struggle is the same as that of the consultant employed in a large firm. Many resolve this dilemma by seeking their own work; others see the advantages of not having to search for work and not having to be totally responsible.

Lone Consultant or Consulting Firm Manager?

*T*hough I've worked alone for thirteen years, I continue to revisit my decision to work for and by myself, which tells you that I'm not resolved about it yet. Here are some of my recurring thoughts and dreams:

- If it is just me, I do not have to check with anyone (at work) on what I decide to do.
- If I were the manager of my own firm, I would have others to talk to about my work, but I also would have to talk to them about where the firm is going.

- If it is just me, I can work part-time, full-time, or double-time and not have to involve others in that decision.
- If I have even one person working for me full-time, my job moves toward full-time too, in the sense of feeling a full-time responsibility for that person.
- As long as I am working by myself, I can work out of my home. When I add one person, or five, this quickly becomes impossible, and I have to rent an office, buy more furniture, and commute to my office—probably in a suit instead of my pajamas (one of my favorite items of office wear).
- Working by myself, I only get paid when I am doing work. If I had a person working for me, I would make money when that person worked. And if I had five people, I could make five times as much.
- If I ran a small firm of six to eight people, we could take on projects much larger than any I can consider now all by myself. We could learn more and earn more.
- As the owner of a consulting business that builds a positive reputation over the years, perhaps with a small line of products as well as consulting services, I could have something that others would be willing to pay for. I could sell the firm and make a few million, maybe.
- As a one-person operation, everything I do involves me. I don't have much to sell to anyone else, should I decide to retire. There is no equity to put on the market.
- A firm with a number of consultants requires full-time support staff. With that comes related equipment: computers, copy machines, fax machines, printers, and so on. There is great advantage to having this human and electronic help close at hand.
- As an individual working alone, I find myself licking stamps, making copies, typing reports, collating pages, paying bills, and performing many other activities that do not use my best talents.

I have talked with many consultants who have struggled to build a firm from a solo practice. Their experience tells me that a consulting firm has to have about eight consultants before the firm's owner begins to have the flexibility he or she had as an individual working alone. Four- to six-person firms seem to be surviving more often than thriving; they are at a critical in-between point in their growth. With about eight consultants, the owner can justify the overhead of an office manager to take some of the burden that the owner has been carrying. It also is at about this point that the owner can begin to profit financially from all the work being done by his or her consultants. So I continue to think about it, and continue to find it much more of a "should do" than a "want to do."

Preparing for This Work

*I*n the third grade I wrote a paper that began, "When I grow up, I want to be a bartender." That is as close as I came to putting myself on the consulting path at an early age. Actually, when I wrote that paper in 1946, I think most consultants *were* bartenders! There is some kinship between the two professions. Today, I meet advanced-degree graduates who apparently have wanted to be consultants since the third grade. They are still the exception; as a rule, we grow into consulting out of related work.

My experience biases me. I have no formal academic preparation to do the work I am doing. And I see many consultants who have built successfully on previous life and work experience, without having strong academic credentials. Most of them didn't plan to be consultants when they started working. I suspect they are better consultants for the diverse experiences they have had.

We are going to see an amazing crop of mature, savvy consultants in a few years, when all of those graduate students in organizational behavior, organizational development, and human resources development have added fifteen years of life and work experience to their schooling. They have the potential to be particularly insightful. They also run the risk of becoming consultants too early. When I read in the *Wall Street Journal* about M.B.A.'s running off to work with consulting firms, I am not encouraged.

One the best ways of preparing to help others in their work is to do that work ourselves for a while. The consultant's role is a step removed from the work. To take that step too early can preclude a deeper understanding of what the work is about. When I hear about a line manager of ten years taking a leave of absence to pursue a master's degree in organizational behavior, that excites me. In this case, life and work experience can be added to education to the benefit of the individual and of future clients.

Conclusion: The Continuing Quest for Meaning Through Work

This book began with "Balance and Being," in which I talked with you about the importance of searching out or creating our meaning in this life. In the next two parts, "Opening the Organization" and "Power and the Partnership," I elaborated on ways of continuing that search as we do our work with our clients. I made "Money and the Marketplace" the last part of the book because I see it as least important—though essential. Like the basement utility room discussed in the Introduction, it is full of tools useful in maintaining a consulting practice. My hope is that you can move beyond maintenance and spend more time upstairs, balancing your work within your life, realizing success, and building strong relationships with clients.

The Preface opened with the question:

> How do you thrive as a consultant,
> contribute to the world,
> make friends, and
> become the person you want to be?

This book's title suggests the short answer: Pursue this work as a personal calling, bringing who you are to what you do. I have reinforced this central theme in many different ways. I have traveled back and forth over the same ground from one direction and then from another, all with the intention of helping you define the kind of consultant you want to be.

Ending this book is like pausing while backpacking on a long, challenging, and beautiful trail. I haven't really finished, because I have not reached a destination. Instead, I am stepping off the trail to rest for awhile, to let others go by, and to reflect on what I have learned so far. The things I have learned from past experiences are much clearer to me than what awaits me around the next curve. I cannot see where this trail leads beyond the next hundred feet or so, but the path always seems to open up just when I think it has run out. I can count on it. That is where the calling comes in.

The best moments I've ever had in this work combine to tell me the following things:

- Find work you love to do and are called to do.
- If consulting is not your calling, then get out of it. Life is too short to spend all those hours on work you do not want to do.
- When your work is your calling, where you are going is even more exciting than where you have been—and it is riskier, even frightening.
- There is no magic way to consult. There is no "only" way, no best way, no right way. You will choose your own way.
- Pay attention to yourself and you will find that you know what to do next. Your experience, awareness, intuition, and common sense combine to tell you what to do. The task is getting everything else out of the way so that you can know what you want to do.
- You will never "arrive"; you will never be the complete consultant. Others may think you have arrived but you will know you have not. There is always more to become. In this work there is no destination worth reaching and settling down in forever.
- Doing this work without love is unfulfilling. Separating love and your work is unnatural. Together they bring fulfillment.

Index

A

Abuses of power, 163–65
Acceptance, leading to love, 29
Accomplishments of consultants and clients, 137–39
Agoraphobia, 179–80
Alternatives for clients' problems
    clients' action on, 79–80
    offered by consultants, 79, 81
Anxieties, 20–22, 39
Articles
    managing resource files, 54–55
    as a marketing tool, 192–94, 220–21
Assessing an organization's problem, 78–79, 80–81
Assessing yourself. *See* Self-assessment
Authenticity
    being versus playing consultant, 19–20
    in consultant-client partnerships, 132–34
    deception of clients by consultants, 170–74
    needing money rather than work, 215–16
    pretension between consultant and client, 149–50, 169–70

B

Balance
    accepting work selectively, 44–47
    how to balance your schedule, 41–44
    of needs in consultant-client partnership, 121–22
    one-person organization versus available jobs, 40–41
    travel versus local work, 47–49
    between work and life, 1–2
    work schedule versus time for yourself, 36–40
    working at home, 50–53
Being yourself. *See* Authenticity
Belcher, Forrest, 53
Beliefs. *See also* Values and vision

acceptance of one's darker self, 22–25
    values as beliefs, 104–105
Block, Peter, xix, xxiv, 214
Books
    managing book collections, 55–56
    writing, 194–96
Brochures and marketing, 190–91
Business cards, note cards, and stationery, 189–90

C

Calling, definition of, xviii–xix
Change in organizations
    consultants as change agents, xxi
    painful nature of, 89
    perseverence of consultants, 96
    simple approach recommended, 85–87
    slowness of, 73
Charging for services. *See* Money
Clients. *See also* Consultant-client partnership; Organizations
    acceptance of a client, 29
    barriers between consultants and, 87–88
    beliefs and values, 104–105
    embracing a client's thoughts and problems, 29, 84–85, 96–98
    envisioning future goals, 105–106
    knowledge of a client's situation, 28
    levels of clients, 46
    local clients, 45
    long-term relationship with clients, 96
    loving your clients, 28–30
    potential clients, 220
    reasons for hiring consultants, xvii–xviii
    risk taking, 89–91
    types of clients, 46
    understanding clients, 28
    unmeasurable nature of life issues, 106–109
    working for friends, 46